AF411802

Cristina Iglesias

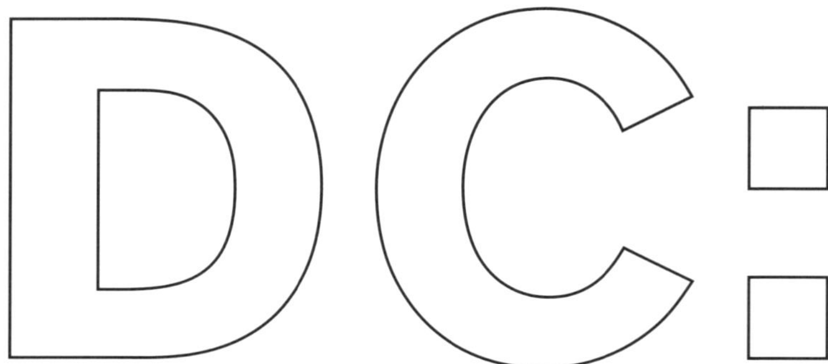

Drei hängende Korridore
Three Suspended Corridors

Cristina Iglesias

Museum Ludwig, Köln

Verlag der Buchhandlung
Walther König, Köln

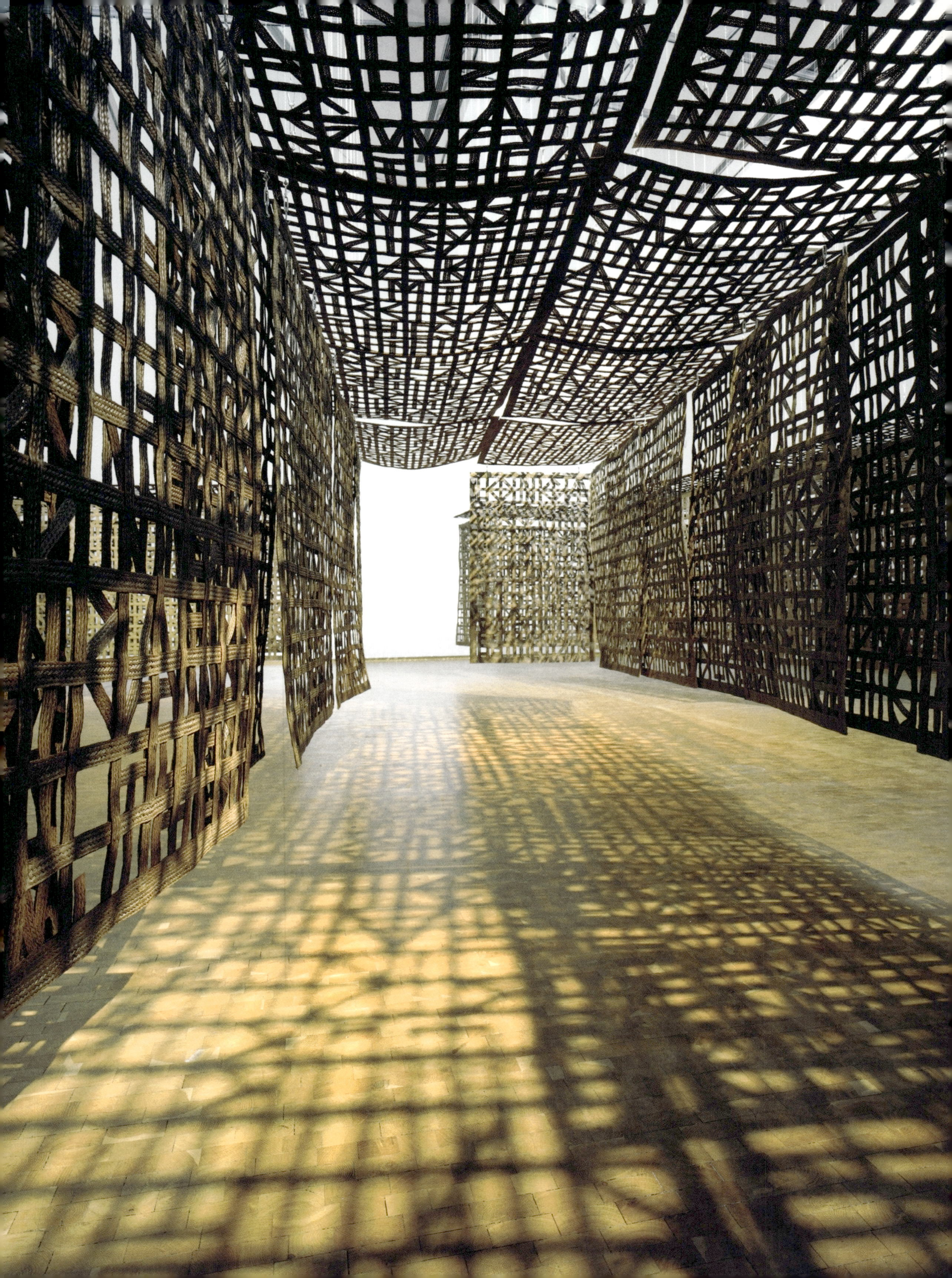

Vorwort

KASPER KÖNIG

Die aktuelle Ausstellung *Drei Hängende Korridore* ist das Resultat eines lange gehegten Projekts von Ulrich Wilmes, der die künstlerische Entwicklung von Cristina Iglesias seit vielen Jahren intensiv verfolgt. Ihr in den frühen 80er Jahren ansetzendes Werk ist gekennzeichnet durch eine komplexe Durchdringung verschiedener künstlerischer Disziplinen, die über ihr eigenes Selbstverständnis als Bildhauerin hinausgreift in die Bereiche von Architektur und Fotografie sowie in einem ganz spezifischen Sinne in das Feld der Literatur. Dieser interdisziplinären Offenheit entspricht ein ebenso weit gefächertes formales Interesse an diversen Materialien, die außerordentlich per se erscheinen und zum Teil in relativ ungewöhnlicher Weise verarbeitet werden. Für die Installation im Museum Ludwig hat Cristina Iglesias eine architektonische Konstruktion geschaffen, die aus einem Geflecht von flachen metallenen Bändern besteht, die galvanisiert und patiniert sind.

Ein wesentlicher Aspekt ihres skulpturalen Konzepts, das in bedächtigen Schritten folgerichtig weiter entwickelt, ist die Beschreibung eines Ortes oder treffender der Vorstellung eines Ortes. Dabei läßt sich Cristina Iglesias von Texten inspirieren, die ebenfalls eine beschreibende Funktion innerhalb einer Erzählung besitzen. Diese Passagen werden von ihr in keiner Weise bildnerisch nachgeahmt. Vielmehr transformiert sie die Vorstellungen, die sich in ihr bei der Lektüre einprägen, völlig unabhängig von deren Inhalt oder Erzählfunktion.

In kuratorischer Zusammenarbeit mit Ulrich Wilmes hat Cristina Iglesias eine beeindruckende Installation geschaffen, die die enorme Dimension des DC:-Saales mit großer Selbstverständlichkeit und Souveränität bewältigt. Ihr gilt an erster Stelle unser herzlicher Dank für die freundschaftliche Zusammenarbeit. Sehr zu Dank verpflichtet bin ich einmal mehr unserem Schreinermeister Armin Lüttgen, der den statisch hoch komplizierten Aufbau geplant, organisiert und umgesetzt hat, wie immer unterstützt durch sein Mitarbeiter-Team und unseren Hausinspektor Ralf Feckler. Dankbar bin ich ebenfalls für die bewährte Kooperation mit der *StadtRevue*, in deren aktueller Ausgabe wiederum ein von der Künstlerin gestaltetes Insert erscheint, das die medial übergreifenden Aspekte im Werk von Cristina Iglesias anschaulich widerspiegelt. Danken möchte ich ferner dem Spanischen Kulturministerium und der Staatlichen Gesellschaft für Kulturförderung im Ausland sowie den Rechtsanwälten Bach, Langheid & Dallmayr für die großzügige Unterstützung dieser Ausstellung. Wie immer endet mein besonderer Dank bei den Mitgliedern des AC:/DC: Förderkreises, die unter der Initiative von Anna Friebe-Reininghaus auch 2006 die Projekte grundsätzlich ermöglichen. Zu nennen sind: Dr. Wolfgang Bornheim, Anna Friebe-Reininghaus, Dr. Dietrich Gottwald und Dr. Wolfgang Strobel.

Preface

KASPER KÖNIG

The current exhibition *Three Suspended Corridors* is the result of a project that has been nurtured for a long time by Ulrich Wilmes who, for many years, has followed the artistic development of Cristina Iglesias with keen interest.

Her work took its beginning in the early 1980s and is characterised by a complex fusion of different artistic disciplines, extending beyond her self-perception as a sculptor into the realms of architecture and photography as well as, in a very specific sense, into the field of literature. Hand in hand with this interdisciplinary openness goes an equally wide-ranging formal interest in diverse materials which seem extraordinary per se and which are at times treated in a relatively unconventional fashion.

For the installation in the Museum Ludwig, Cristina Iglesias has created an architectonic construction consisting of a latticework of flat metal ribbons, which have been galvanised and patinated. A fundamental aspect of her sculptural concept, developed consistently in judicious steps, is the description of a place or, more precisely, the notion of a place. During this process Cristina Iglesias takes her inspiration from texts fragments which, within their story, also have a descriptive function. However, she does not in any way attempt to recreate these passages sculpturally. Instead, she transforms the images that form in her mind whilst she reads, wholly independent of their content or narrative function.

In curatorial collaboration with Ulrich Wilmes Cristina Iglesias has created an impressive installation, which handles the enormous dimension of the DC:- room with great genuineness and spontaneity. First and foremost we would like to thank her wholeheartedly for her genial collaboration. Once again I am deeply indebted to our carpenter Armin Lüttgen, who planned, organised and realised the statically complex construction, as always assisted by his team and our janitor Ralf Feckler. I am also grateful for the unfailing cooperation of the *StadtRevue*, in whose current edition an insert designed by the artist has been published, clearly reflecting the cross media aspects of Cristina Iglesias' work. I am also obliged to the Spanish Ministry of Culture and the State Corporation for Spanish Cultural Action Abroad as well as the Bach, Langheid & Dallmayr legal practice for their generous support of this exhibition. As always, I would like to finish by extending my special thanks to the Friends of the AC:/DC: room, who, under the initiative of Anna Friebe-Reininghaus, also make these projects fundamentally possible in 2006. In this context I would like to mention Dr Wolfgang Bornheim, Anna Friebe-Reininghaus, Dr Dietrich Gottwald and Dr Wolfgang Strobel.

Die Dramatisierung des Raumes
Cristina Iglesias *Drei hängende Korridore*, 2006

ULRICH WILMES

I.

Die Wände und das Dach der Gasse, in die wir als Besucher hineingehen, umgeben uns mit rechteckigen Gittern oder Matten aus einem metallenen Flechtwerk, welche die Wände und Dächer bilden. Sie sind von der Decke eines Umraumes abgehängt. Über dem Boden schwebend sind sie einer statischen Fixierung entzogen. Die formale Erscheinung dieser Gebilde ist außergewöhnlich und es fällt schwer eine griffige Bezeichnung anzugeben, die sie eindeutig beschreibt. Diese anschauliche Schwierigkeit hat zunächst mit ihrem Material zu tun. Sie bestehen aus einer Vielzahl kleiner Stränge, die aus dünnstem Draht gebündelt zu flachen Bändern geflochten sind. Das galvanisierte Eisen ist patiniert, wodurch dem Geflecht eine gealterte Erscheinung verliehen wird.

In den *Drei hängenden Korridoren* sind die oberen Matten schematisch aneinandergefügt, während die seitlichen unregelmäßig aufgereiht sind. Sie überlappen sich häufig in mehreren Schichten, um die unvermeidlichen Abstände zwischen ihnen zu überbrücken, und erscheinen so in ihrem Verlauf jeweils dichter oder transparenter. Das Licht dringt folglich in unterschiedlicher Intensität ein und wird durch die komplizierte Struktur der Matten in einem verwirrenden Schattenspiel zerhackt. Ihre strukturelle Basis besteht aus Quadraten. Auf oder besser in dieses karierte Maschenwerk eingeschrieben stehen Buchstaben und Worte, die kaum zu entziffern sind. Die Schriftzeichen sind in das stabilisierende Raster integriert und gehen mit ihrer Schreibunterlage eine rätselhafte Verbindung

ein. Zudem verstellen die Matten an vielen Stellen durch ihre Überlappung die unmittelbare Lesbarkeit. Die Besucher, sobald sie auf die Textfragmente stoßen, fühlen sich herausgefordert, ihren Inhalt zu entschlüsseln und einen Zusammenhang herzustellen, von dem sie sich eine Erklärung versprechen. Bald werden sie sich allerdings der Schwierigkeit, wenn nicht der Vergeblichkeit seines Bemühens stellen müssen.

Mit dem Eintritt in den Raum bewegen sich die Besucher in einer fremdartigen Welt. An ihrer

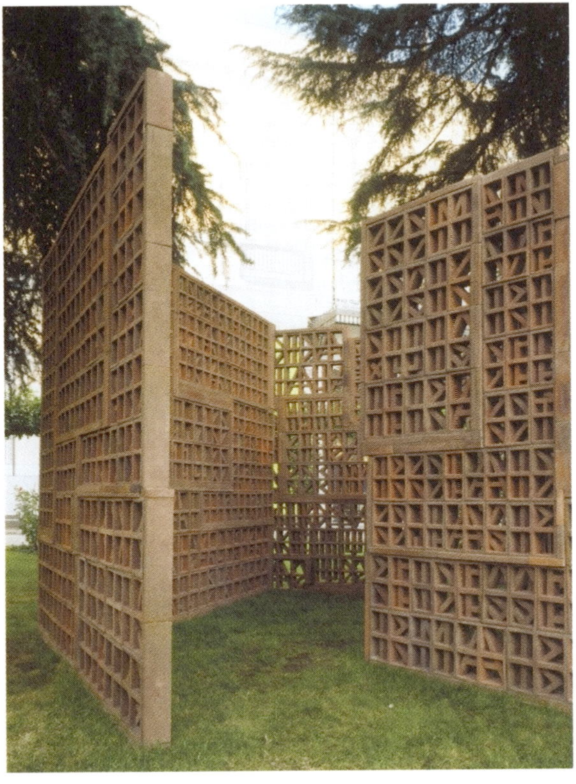

Ohne Titel (Celosía IX), 2005. Ton, 560 x 480 cm, Sammlung Plácido Arango (Foto: Luis Asin)

Schwelle stehend öffnet sich uns eine unbekannte Zone, von der wir nicht wissen können, was sich in ihr verbirgt. Die Gasse verspricht den Aufbruch zu neuen Erfahrungen und Eindrücken. Ungewißheit und Rätsel begleiten uns auf diesem Weg, dessen Verlauf nicht zu überblicken und dessen Ziel nicht zu erkennen ist. Noch können wir unsere Verweildauer vorhersagen, fest steht nur, daß wir bei der Entdeckung auf uns selbst gestellt sind. „Die Abfolge des Anschauens beinhaltet eine Navigation durch Raum und Zeit als ein kompositionelles Element, das dem Prozeß des Sehens und Erfahrens der Skulptur innewohnt. Durch ein Werk zu gehen, sei es physisch oder mental, berücksichtigt diese zeitlichen Komponenten."[1]

II.

Aus früheren Werke von Cristina Iglesias kennen wir vergleichbare gitterartige Strukturen aus unterschiedlichen Materialien, deren vielgestaltige Arabesken an die maurischen Paläste der Alhambra erinnern und deren fragmentarische Texte wie Hieroglyphen zu uns sprechen. Es gehört zu den bemerkenswerten Eigenschaften ihres Werks, das bestimmte formale und inhaltliche Motive in einem langsamen Fluß kontinuierlicher Entwicklung weitergetragen werden.

Die *Korridore* kombinieren Elemente zweier Werkgruppen. Zum einen greift die Künstlerin ihre seit Ende der 90er Jahre entstandenen *Celosías / Jalousien* (1996/97) auf, deren filigran gearbeiteten Kabinette aus verschachtelten Gitterwerken bestehen. Diese sind aus Holz und Kunstharz gebaut, das mit Bronzepuder patiniert wird. Mit ihrem Titel verweisen sie auf die Struktur arabischer Fenstergitter, die den Blick von innen nach außen erlauben, aber umgekehrt den Einblick in den Raum verwehren. Gleichzeitig spielt diese Bezeichnung auf eine erweiterte Bedeutung des Wortes an, das im Spanischen und Französischen auch für Eifersucht steht. Zum anderen verweisen sie auf die jüngeren *Pasajes / Passagen* (seit 2002), deren ähnlich strukturierte Matten aus Esparto gefertigt sind, eine bastähnliche Naturfaser, die in Südeuropa und Nordafrika zu unterschiedlichen

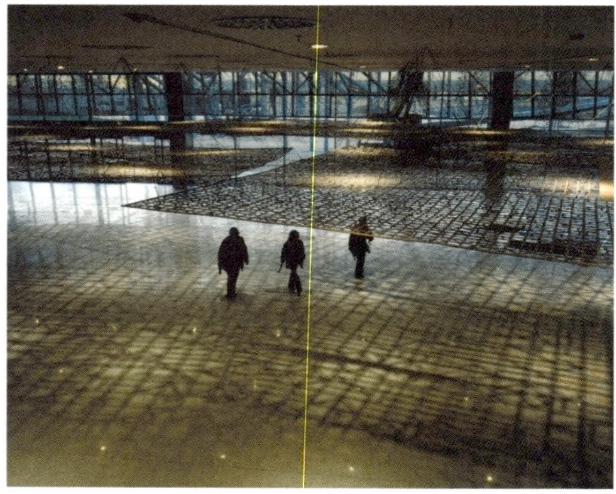

Permanente Installation für das internationale Kongresszentrum Barcelona, 2004. Geflochtener Draht, Stahlkabel, 17 Teile, je 1300 x 900 cm, gesamt: 15000 x 3000 cm (Foto: Kristien Daem)

Gebrauchsgegenständen verarbeitet wird. Unter anderem dient sie zum Flechten von Überdachungen, wie sie in arabischen Basaren zum Schutz vor der brennenden Sonne angebracht werden und hier wie dort ein flirrendes Wechselspiel von Licht und Schatten im Raum erzeugen.

Vor geraumer Zeit, als sie noch mit der Ausarbeitung der Idee beschäftigt war, lieferte Iglesias bereits eine genaue Beschreibung des entstehenden Werks als weiterentwickelte Variation der vorangegangenen *Jalousien* und *Passagen*. Darin spricht sie davon, daß die von der Decke hängenden Matten, einen „Durchgang [gestalten], der irgendwo in einem weißen Raum endet". Zugleich betont sie die Funktion des Lichts, das „von oben auf die Arbeit [fällt] und den Schatten von Texten auf den Boden wirft". Während also der Betrachter durch die überdachte Gasse geht, „fallen die Schatten der Texte uns zu Füßen; wir sind über und unter dem Werk zur selben Zeit. Wenn wir nach oben sehen, ist die Überdachung gleichzeitig transparent und durch Worte verdichtet, und bietet eine Ansicht, die nichts mit Skulptur zu tun hat."[2] Iglesias stellt also klar, daß die skulpturale Gestalt der *Korridore* allein über die polyperspektivische Wahrnehmung von Raum, Objekt und Schrift zu erschließen ist. Damit rücken einerseits der Plan der Anlage und andererseits die literarischen Verweise in das Blickfeld der Besucher.

8

III.

Die Anlage der *Korridore* besteht aus drei Flügeln, die in den Raum eingreifen. Nachdem die Besucher den ersten durchschritten haben, befinden sie sich im ungefähren Zentrum des Plans, von wo aus zwei weitere gleicher Machart, aber mit unterschiedlichem Grundriß, erreichbar sind. An diesem zentralen Ort gewinnen wir einen Eindruck der äußeren Gestalt der Anlage und erkennen ihre Positionierung innerhalb des umgebenden Raumes. Die von den Bauteilen eingefaßten Zonen können als räumlicher Wechsel zwischen Innen- und Außen erfahren werden. Dabei werden hier keine negativ eingeschlossenen Resträume ausgewiesen, als vielmehr Plätze, die sich außerhalb der festgelegten Gassen befinden. Die Besucher werden also die gesamte Anlage in ihrer Analogie zu einer urbanen Landschaft erleben, deren labyrinthische Desorientierung aus besetzten und unbesetzten Räumen erwächst. „Mich interessiert dieser glückliche Zwang, der die urbane Landschaft bestimmt. Sie als ein System von Zeichen zu benutzen, die man entziffern kann wie Hieroglyphen – Kodes, die Zeit und Aufmerksamkeit erfordern, um entziffert zu werden. Es liegt niemals eine dekorative Absicht im Gebrauch dieser Zeichen; vielmehr geschieht eine Manipulation jener Mechanismen der Konstruktion und Ornamentierung, um einen Ort der Darstellung zu schaffen."[3]

Die außergewöhnliche Situation des überdimensionalen Ausstellungsraumes wird durch seine Lage innerhalb des Museums bestimmt. Wie eingelassen in seinen architektonischen Kontext erhebt sich der ca. 300 m² große Saal über vier gestaffelte Etagen und ist von einer hohen Empore einzusehen. Von dort können die Besucher die *Korridore* überblicken. Wir sehen durch den „Vorhang" der zahllosen Drähte, an denen die Matten hängen, und auf die flachen „Dächer", die ihm den Grundriß und die Ausdehnung der Anlage, die den gesamten Raum durchmisst, zeigen. Dieser Überblick verwehrt indessen den Einblick in die Gassen und entzieht die darin Anwesenden, die den eingelassenen Beschreibungen übergeben sind, der Beobachtung. Gegenseitiger Augenmerk findet nur außerhalb von ihnen statt.

Doch zurück zum Zentrum der Anlage, wo sich die *Korridore* treffen. Hier kann sich die Spannung der Besucher lösen, die sich durch den vorgewiesenen Durchgang aufgebaut hat. Diese verfliegt mit dem Erreichen eines Platzes, an dem wir uns gleichsam wiederfinden, insofern wir unsere Orientierung zurückgewinnen. Wir bemerken, das die labyrinthische Einbildung, der wir unterlegen sind, nicht wirklich eingelöst wird. Seit der Antike wird das Labyrinth als Vorstellung eines Bauwerks von seiner umgangssprachlichen und literarischen Deutung überlagert, die sich von seiner eigentlichen Gestalt unterscheidet. Diese entwirft eine komplizierte Bewegungsfigur, die einen Innenraum von der Außenwelt abgrenzt. Ein einziger Zugang weist auf den alleinigen Weg, der in einem pendelartigen Wechsel der Bewegungsrichtung zwangsläufig zum Zentrum führt, wo der Besucher sich eingeschlossen findet. Dieser Logik der Anlage folgend bleibt als Ausgang nur die Umkehr und Rückverfolgung des Wegs, der ihn zuvor hineingeführt hat. In Iglesias' Installation wird das labyrinthische System als Gedankengebäude angedeutet, dessen Zugänglichkeit durch die integrierten Textfragmente erschwert wird. Dies rührt daher, daß die „… Erzählung ein Eigenleben [gewinnt], das sich von den Bildern wegbewegt, bis wir verloren sind. Der einzige Weg, sich selbst wieder zu finden, ist, zwei Straßen gleichzeitig zu gehen. Oder, in den Worten des amerikanischen Baseballspielers Yogi Berra: ,Wenn Du an eine Weggabelung kommst, folge

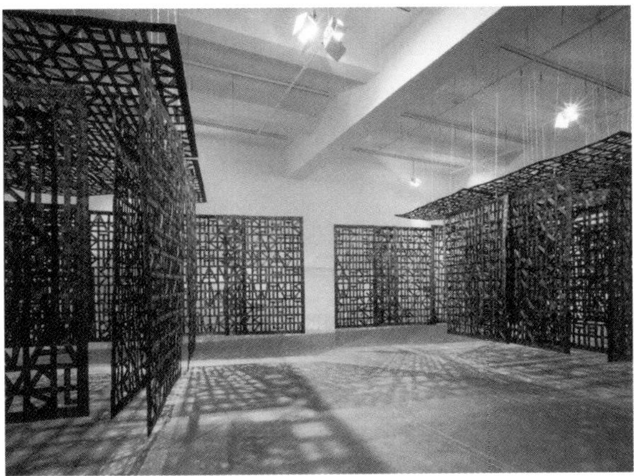

Pavillon I und II in einem Raum hängend, 2005. Geflochtener Draht, Stahlkabel, 50 Teile, 185 x 120 cm, Pavillon I, Tate Gallery, London (Foto: Attilio Maranzano)

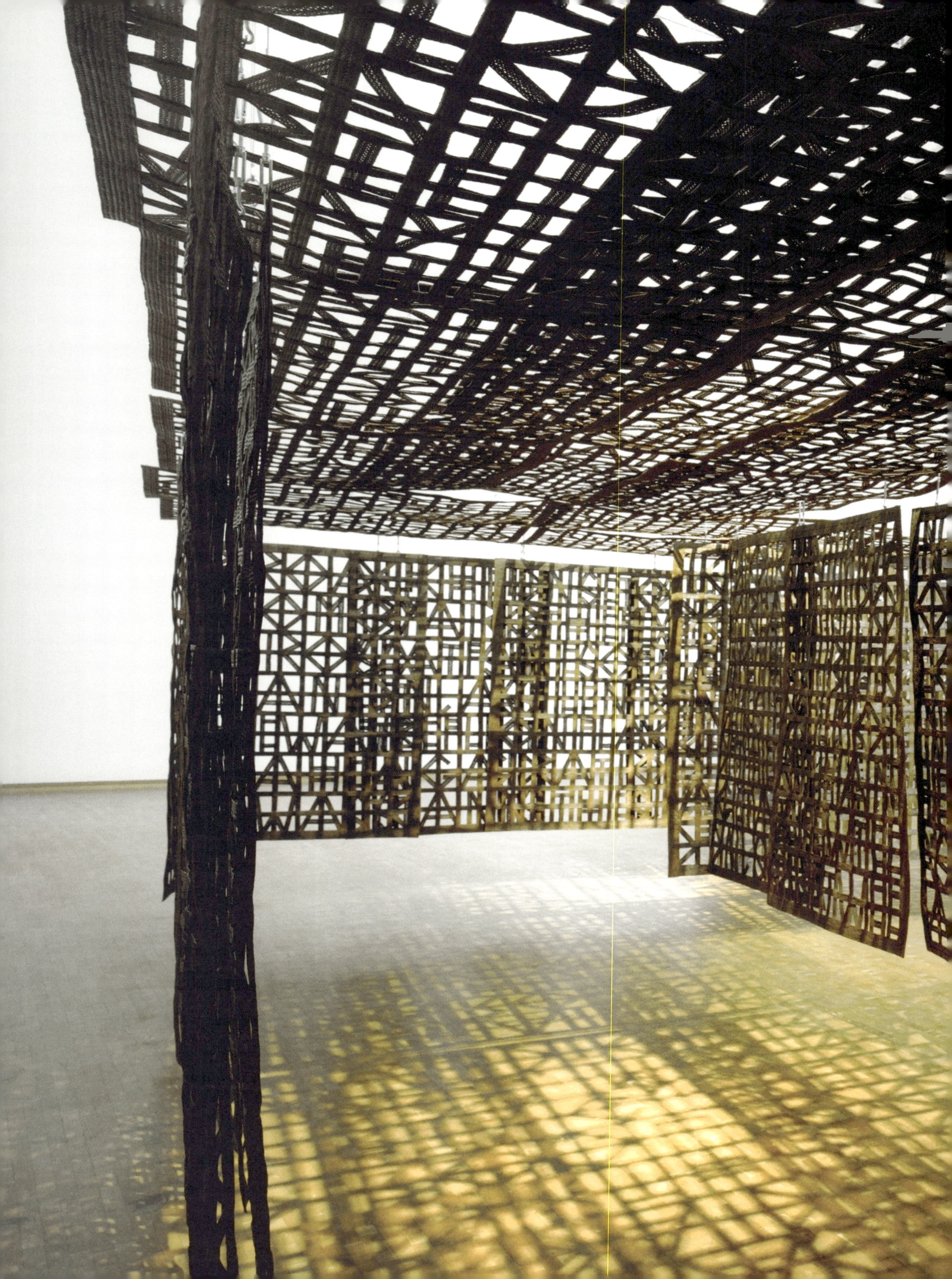

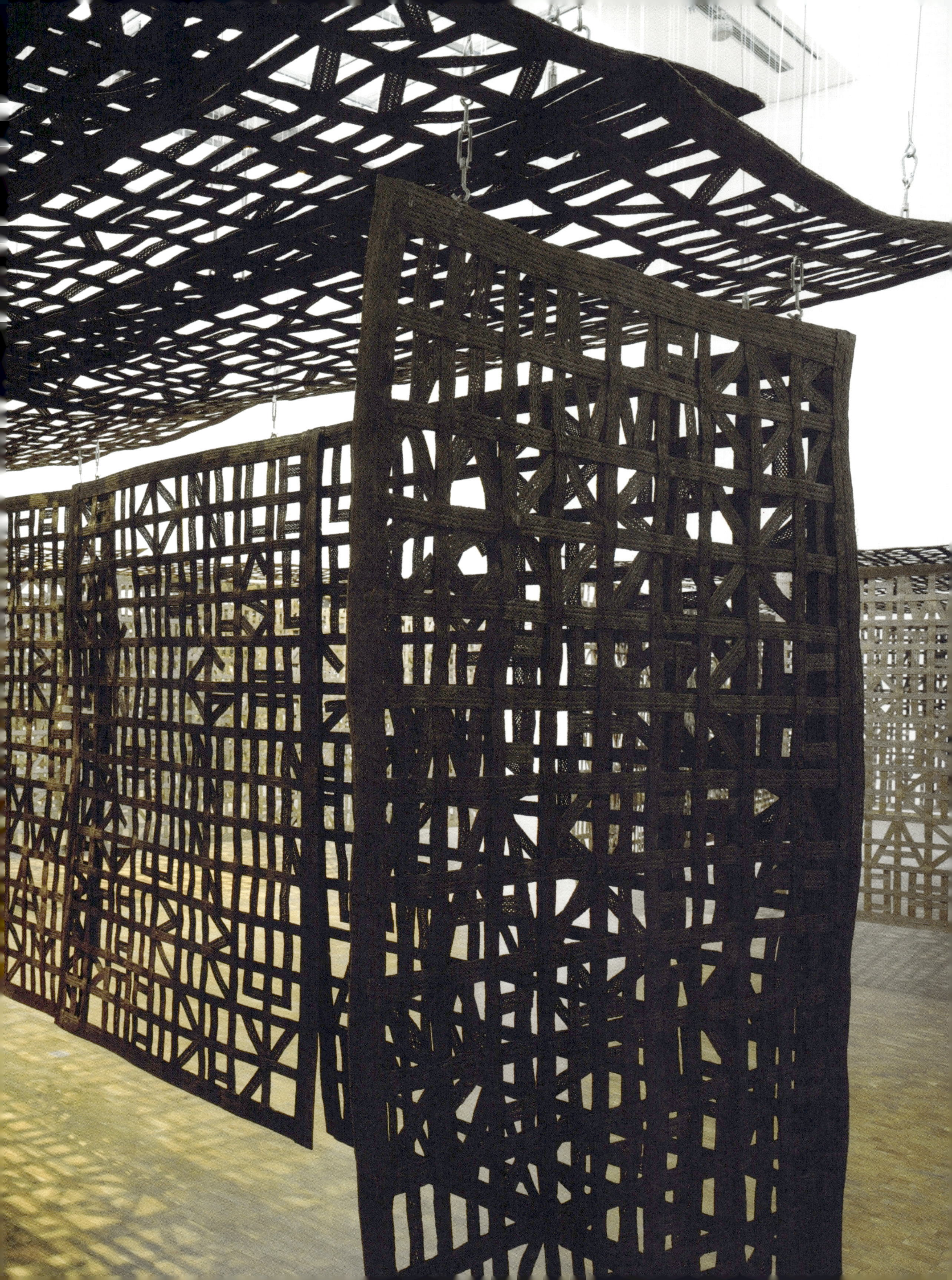

ihr!"[4] In Iglesias' räumlichen „Erfindungen"
scheinen diese imaginierten Räume als Anleihe
aus literarischen Quellen auf, deren Ursprung
die Künstlerin nicht vorenthält. In Interviews
hat sie auf die verwendeten Texte verwiesen,
und in Katalogen sind sie zitiert. Dabei zielt die
bildnerische Strategie auf eine vergleichende
Lesbarkeit der unterschiedlichen visuellen Gegebenheiten. Das Warum und die Weise ihrer Ver-
wendung von Texten aus Joris-Karl Huysmans'
A Rebours und Raymond Roussels *Impressions
d'Afrique* in vorherigen Werken ist bereits im
Rahmen früherer Ausstellungen ausführlich behandelt worden. Sie beruhen auf der Auseinan-
dersetzung mit einer analogen „Idee der ‚Erfindung'", die einen Raum hervorbringt, „der niemals existiert hat". Iglesias geht es um die Beschreibung eines solches Ortes „innerhalb eines
anderen Raumes", der den Besucher mit seinen
statischen Bauteilen und eingefügten Schriftzeichen einkreist. „Die Beschreibung eines vor-
gestellten Gartens mit einer Spur sowohl wirk-
licher, gelebter Erfahrung als auch reiner Phan-
tasie. In den Gittern ist die Rekonstruktion des
Textes ein Bestandteil des Werks und bedeutet
zugleich eine Unmöglichkeit. Die Fragmentie-
rung des Textes bürdet eine ausgedehnte, aus-
geweitete Zeit auf, die schwer nachzuvollziehen,
geschweige denn zu ertragen ist. Dies würde
passieren, wenn wir in einem Raum mit Hieroglyphen an allen Wänden eingeschlossen wären.
Es ist weniger meine Absicht einzuschließen als
zu umschließen. Innerhalb solcher Arbeiten gibt
es eine Vorstellung des Aufzeichnens, die eine
Strategie der Bewegung erfordert. Als ob man
verloren wäre."[5]

IV.

Mit der Entdeckung der Schrift bewegen sich die
Besucher nicht mehr nur in einem skulpturalen
Werk, sondern zugleich und mehr noch in einem
beschriebenen wie beschreibenden Raum. Die
Verflechtung aus statischem Gerüst und flüch-
tiger Bedeutung folgt einer formalen Strategie,
welche die nach Autonomie strebende Form mit
bildsprachlichen Fragmenten verdichtet. Ihre
„Textur" erscheint hier in wörtlicher Auslegung
ihres lateinischen Wortsinns tatsächlich als

„kunstvolles Gewebe", das die Besucher in
einem unentdeckten Raum isoliert. Die aufge-
gebenen Rätsel sind allein aus der diesseitigen
Anschauung nicht zu entschlüsseln, sondern for-
dern in hohem Grade die jenseitige Vorstellung
heraus. Sie werden kaum greifbar in der Anwe-
senheit der durchbrochenen Begrenzungen des
Gitterwerks aufgrund der gleichzeitigen Abwe-
senheit eines Verständnisses der fragmentari-
schen Schriften. Das heißt, der Konzeption des
skulpturalen Werks wohnt eine Dialektik von
geschlossener Form und offener Deutung inne,
die zugleich als Wirklichkeit und Fiktion wahr-
genommen wird. Wer sich in diesen Raum
hineinbegibt, ist der zeitlichen Linearität von
Vergangenheit, Gegenwart und Zukunft entzogen.

Die *Korridore* sind eine erweiterte Entwick-
lungsstufe zu den *Pavillons*, die im vergangenen
Jahr 2005 entstanden sind. Diese sind aus den
gleichen rechteckigen Matten aus metallenem
Flechtwerk gefertigt und hängen ebenfalls von
der Decke des Raumes herab. Ihr Grundriß ist
rechteckig, und ihr Aufbau erinnert an die Leich-
tigkeit japanischer Häuser – eine Allusion, die
wiederum die Ahnung eines ganz spezifisches
Systems von bildhaften Schriftzeichen mit sich
trägt. Gleichwohl vermitteln sie ein statisches
Prinzip örtlicher Fixierung, das sie mit den
Jalousien verbindet und trotz ihrer Transparenz
eine Empfindung von Eingeschlossenheit in
sich birgt.

Als literarischer Bezugsrahmen diente Iglesias
der Science-Fiction-Roman *Rendezvous with
Rama* von Arthur C. Clarke aus dem Jahre 1973.
Er behandelt einen klassischen Topos des Genres,
das erste Zusammentreffen der Menschheit mit
einer außerirdischen Intelligenz. Es manifestiert
sich in der Begegnung mit einem Raumkörper
von gigantischen Ausmaßen, der mit unbekann-
ter Herkunft und unbekanntem Ziel unsere
Galaxie kreuzt. Nur wenige Tage bleiben der
Besatzung eines Raumschiffs, das unter der
Nummer 31/439 mit dem Namen „Rama" regis-
trierte Flugobjekt zu untersuchen. Die Erkun-
dung bestätigt die aus der Distanz gewonnene
Vermutung, daß es einem perfekt geformten
Zylinder mit einer Länge von ca. 50 Kilometern
entspricht. Als die Besatzung darauf landet und
in den Raumkörper eindringt, öffnet sich ihr

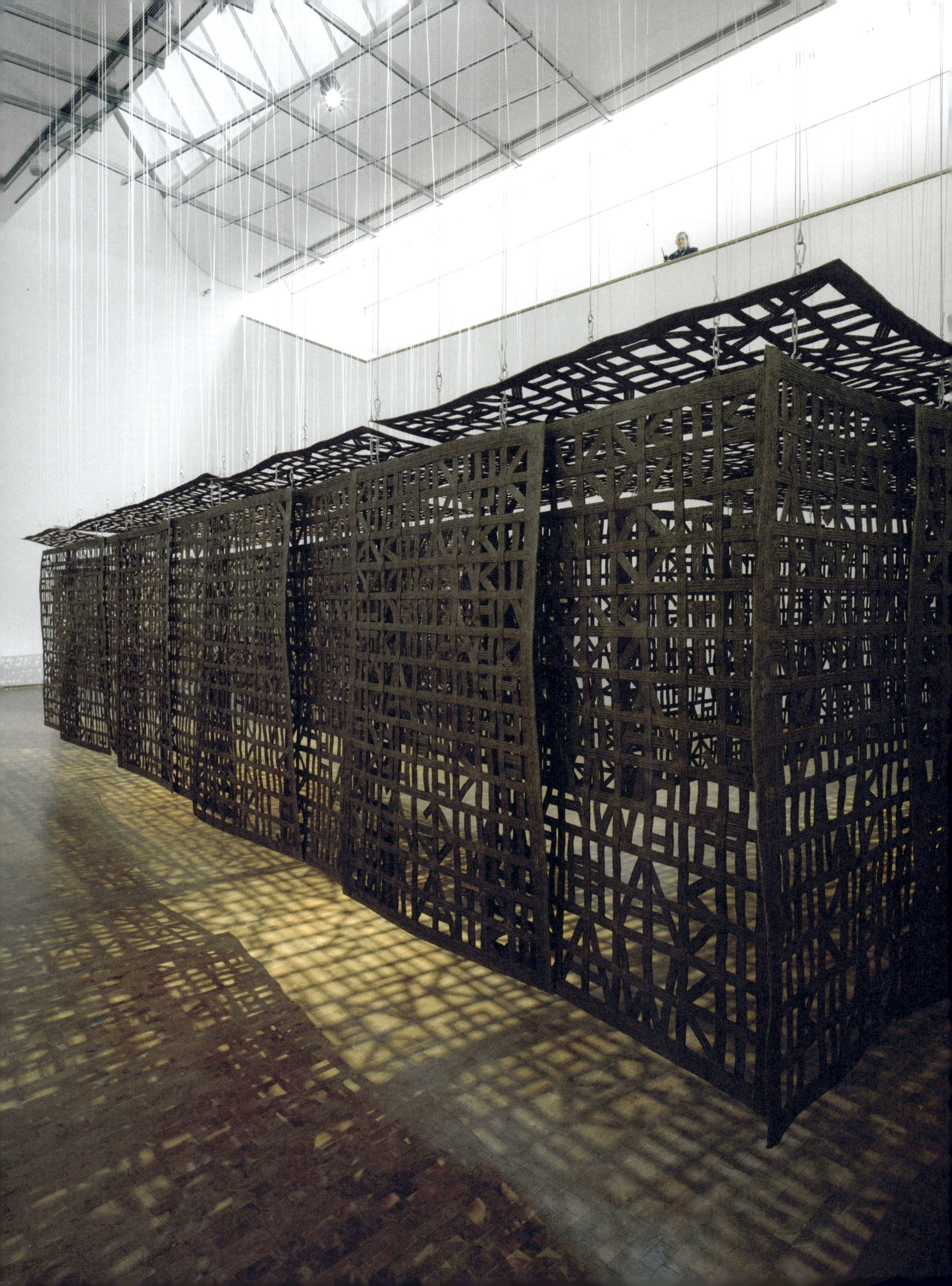

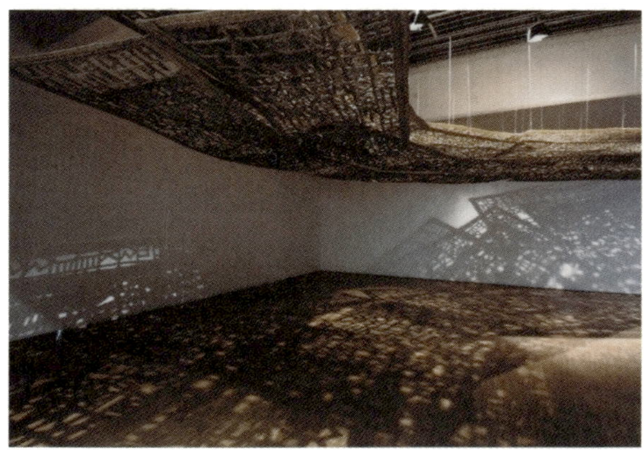

Ohne Titel (Passage II), 2005. Raffiabast,
300 x 125 cm, Centre Georges Pompidou, Paris
(Foto: Georges Méguerdichian)

eine bizarre Welt, die wie ein surreales techni-
sches Kunstwerk erscheint. Je weiter die Raum-
fahrer und Wissenschaftler in diesen faszinie-
renden künstlichen Raum vordringen, desto
mehr sind sie ergriffen von seiner wundersamen
Erscheinung, die mehr Fragen aufwirft als Ant-
worten bereithält. Clarke hat mit *Rama* einen
Mythos geschaffen, der sich beinahe verselb-
ständigt hat. Die Hauptrolle darin nehmen
nicht etwa die heldenhaften Eindringlinge ein,
sondern der Gegenstand ihrer abenteuerlichen
Mission, dieser unvorstellbare Raumkörper und
seine autarke Welt.

Es steht außer Frage, daß es Iglesias nicht
um eine wörtliche Übertragung von Clarkes uto-
pischen Visionen in eine bildnerische Sprache
geht. Seine literarische Erfindung einer unbeleb-
ten außerirdischen Welt entspringt reiner Phan-
tasie, deren wahre Gestalt im Verborgenen
bleibt. *Rama* ist ein Mikrokomos, der durch
seine Weite und Vielfalt überwältigt. Sein künst-
licher Himmelskörper weist eine innere Voll-
kommenheit auf, die jenseits der menschlichen
Natur angesiedelt ist. Gleichzeitig vermittelt er
den Eindruck von Verlassenheit und Leere. So
bergen seine sagenhaften Landschaftsräume
auch eine ausgedehnte wie ein Schachbrett
gemusterte Region, deren einzelne Felder mit
Dingen von unterschiedlichster Form, Struktur
und Materialität bestellt sind. Sie wirken auf
den Eindringling wie das Ramanische „Kunst-
museum", bei dessen Besichtigung er unter
anderem Phänomene wie „Teppiche [...] aus ver-
knüpften Drähten" und „zeltartige Gebilde aus

Maschendraht [...] wie gewaltige Vogelkäfige"
entdeckt. Es sind diese Beschreibungen abstrak-
ter Formvorstellungen, die allein durch die
Einbildungskraft begrenzt werden, in denen sich
die bildende Künstlerin wiedergefunden hat.[6]

V.

Die bezeichnende Veränderung der *Drei hängenden Korridore* besteht in der Dynamisierung
ihrer Anlage. Ihre räumliche Ausdehnung bricht
die Hermetik der *Pavillons* auf zugunsten eines
Umschlossenseins, das eine Zielrichtung vorgibt.
In diesem Sinne stellen sie Konstruktionen aus
skulpturalen, architektonischen und literarischen Motiven und Zeichen dar, die aus der
Deutung einer labyrinthischen Bewegungsfigur
abgeleitet werden können. Die räumliche Disposition der drei *Korridore* nimmt allerdings
keinen unmittelbaren Bezug auf die Formprin-
zipien des Labyrinths. Vielmehr scheint seine
Vorstellung die Gestalt zu überlagern und mit
einem gedanklichen Schleier zu überziehen.
In der mythologischen und literarischen Überlie-
ferung wird das Labyrinth meist als verlockende
Falle dargestellt, in der sich der Eintretende ver-
liert und zu Grunde geht. Diese wird im Wesent-
lichen bestimmt durch die angstvolle Vorstellung des isolierten Besuchers von dem, was er
am Ende des Weges am unbekannten Ort findet. Dort wird er letztlich einer Leere begegnen,
die ihn allein mit sich läßt im Bewußtsein seiner
Sterblichkeit.

Die drei Flügel der Anlage beinhalten jeweils
einen zusammenhängenden Textabschnitt, dessen Sätze und Teilsätze in den Matten folgerichtig aufgereiht stehen. Sie sind J.G. Ballards
phantastischem Roman *Kristallwelt* entnommen.
Darin beschreibt er die Bedrohung einer afrika-
nischen Dschungelregion durch einen geheim-
nisvollen Kristallisationsprozeß, der die gesamte
organische wie anorganische Materie in einer
wundersamen Erstarrung sterben läßt. Aus ihrem
Inneren dringt ein eigenartiges Leuchten, das die
Düsternis des tropischen Regenwaldes durch-
strahlt. Die berückende Schönheit der bizarren
Transformation übt eine suggestive Anziehung
auf die Protagonisten der Erzählung aus, der sie
sich nicht entziehen können oder wollen.

14

Iglesias beschränkt ihre „Lektüre" abermals
auf die Beschreibungen der artifiziellen Phänomene des Ortes, die Erscheinung einer durch
Kristallisation und prismatisches Licht verfrem-
deten Umwelt. Sie klammert die Erzählung aus
und übernimmt die Darstellungen der fakti-
schen Gegebenheiten. Weder die Personen und
ihre schicksalhafte Verbindung noch der Hand-
lungsverlauf sind von Interesse. Die Künstlerin
filtert nur Textfragmente heraus, die den Büh-
nenaufbau für das Szenario bilden. Die eingän-
gige Schlichtheit der Beschreibungen der über-
natürlichen Vorgänge ist allerdings kennzeich-
nend für Ballards Erzählstil. Sie macht diese zu
den bemerkenswertesten und nachhaltigsten
Abschnitten des Romans, deren Symbolträch-
tigkeit Iglesias adaptiert. Der Weg in die vom
Kristallisationsprozeß befallene Region führt
über einen Fluß, der „von den hohen Mauern des
Dschungels" eingefaßt wird, die sich im „langge-
zogenen Bogen der Bäume" über die Wasser-
oberfläche wölben. Wie in einem „verschwom-
menen Kaleidoskop" spiegeln sich in ihr „die
überlappenden Farbstreifen" einer Vegetation,
über der „wie eine Kruste das funkelnde Gitter"
liegt. Es ist ein verzauberter Ort, durch den eine
Straße führt, die „zu einem Tunnel gelben und
scharlachroten Lichts geworden war, den das
Blätterdach des Dschungels oben bildet" und
deren „Kristallboden" wie aus „Dornen aus
Basalt" besteht.[7] In Ballards *Kristallwelt* betreten
die Protagonisten eine unwirkliche Zone, in der
die Zeit zum Stillstand gekommen ist und das
Leben in wunderbarer Versteinerung erstarrt, wo
„die menschliche Existenz und das stetige
Suchen ... ein fragwürdiges Ziel und einen be-
klemmenden Abschluß gefunden" haben.[8]

Die Besucher der *Drei Hängenden Korridore*
bewegen sich in einer labyrinthischen Gasse,
die uns mit Zeichen umgibt. Buchstaben lenken
unsere Aufmerksamkeit auf deren Symbolik von
Mitteilung und Verständigung. Wir sind einge-
woben in eine bildnerische Fiktion, wie zurück-
verwiesen auf eine längst verschollene ferne
Zukunft. Ihr beschreibendes Wesen bewirkt, daß
sich hinter dem sehenden Auge der Besucher
ein Raum ausdehnt, der ihn genauso beschäftigt
wie das, was sich sichtbar davor abspielt. Wir
„möchten durch die Gitterwände hindurch-
schauen, [werden] aber aus dem Bild gehalten,

dessen Komponente ... [wir] bereits geworden"
sind. Deshalb erkennen wir letztlich nur das,
was wir mit uns tragen. Für einen Moment ver-
harren wir in der Haltung des Archäologen, der
Grabstätten einer in ferner Vergangenheit ver-
sunkenen Kultur erforscht, um zu verstehen ...!
Allerdings befinden wir uns auf einer grundver-
schiedenen Zeitreise. Während jener den raum-
zeitlichen Kontext der Gegenwart in die Vergangenheit verlagert, bewegen sich die Besucher
der *Korridore* in der Zeitschleife einer sich unbe-
stimmt ausdehnenden Gegenwart. Die Künstlerin will uns darin überzeugen, daß wir es nur
lange genug versuchen müssen, um letztlich
die hieroglyphischen Zeichen entschlüsseln und
deuten zu können. In Iglesias Formulierung, er-
schafft sie eine „Illusion auf der Schwelle zur
Realität", die die Besucher einen Augenblick
lang für wahr halten. Dieser „winzige, allererste
Moment der Täuschung" ist der Ausgangspunkt,
von dem aus „die Reise [... in ein inneres Labyrinth ...] beginnt" – sowohl für die Künstlerin als
auch für die Besucher, die die Präsenz des Werks
als Dramatisierung des Raumes erfahren. Darin
dienen die *Korridore* als Antennen, mit denen
„Entsprechungen, Referenzen, Verflechtungen
und Reflexionen" empfangen werden können,
durch die wir die Wahrheit über uns selbst
wiederfinden.[9]

Anmerkungen

1 Cristina Iglesias im Gespräch mit Gloria Moure, in:
Cristina Iglesias, hrsg. von Iwona Blazwick, Katalog:
Museu Serralves, Porto; Whitechapel Art Gallery, London;
Irish Museum of Modern Art, Dublin; Ediciones Poligrafa,
Barcelona 2002, S. 23.

2 ebd. S. 26.

3 ebd. S. 50.

4 Michael Tarantino, Cristina Iglesias: Between the Natural
and the Artificial, in: *Cristina Iglesias,* hrsg. von Iwona
Blazwick, S. 97/98.

5 Cristina Iglesias, interview with Gloria Moure, in: *Cristina
Iglesias,* hrsg. von Iwona Blazwick, S. 50/57.

6 Arthur C. Clarke, *Rendezvous mit 31/349,* Düsseldorf 1975,
S. 173/175.

7 J.G. Ballard, *Kristallwelt,* Bellheim 2005, S. 65/85.

8 Rezension J.G. Ballard, *Kristallwelt* von Thomas Harbach,
18. September 2005, auf sf_fan.de.

9 Cristina Iglesias im Gespräch mit Doris von Drathen, in:
Künstler – Kritisches Lexikon der Gegenwartskunst,
Ausgabe 59, Heft 17, München 2002, S. 14.

The Dramatization of Space
Cristina Iglesias *Three Suspended Corridors*, 2005

ULRICH WILMES

I.

The visitor enters into an enclosed passageway where rectangular lattices or mats, made of metal tracery, surround him, forming walls and canopies. Suspended from the ceiling of an enclosure they float above the floor, devoid of all static anchoring. The formal appearance of these structures is unusual and makes it hard to find an appropriate terminology which describes them unambiguously. This descriptive difficulty is initially due to the material they are made of. They consist of a multitude of small, flat strands, themselves bundles of thin wire, woven into flat ribbons. The galvanised metal has been patinated, lending the tracery a weathered appearance.

In *Three Suspended Corridors* the upper mats are joined schematically whilst the side ones are hung in irregular rows. Their various layers overlap frequently, bridging the inevitable gaps between them and appearing at times denser or more transparent. Consequently the light permeates them with varying intensity and is lacerated by the complicated structure of the mats, producing a confusing interplay of shadows. The structural basis of these mats is made up of squares. Barely decipherable letters and words are written on, or rather in, this checked network. The characters, integrated in the stabilising grid, enter into a mysterious relationship with the surface they are written on. In addition the overlapping of the mats impairs immediate legibility in many places. The visitor who chances upon such fragments of text will feel challenged to unravel their meaning and put

them in a context, hoping that this will provide some sort of explanation. Soon enough, however, he will have to face up to the difficulty, if not futility of his endeavours.

Upon entering the space the visitor enters a strange world. Standing at its threshold, an unfamiliar territory reveals itself to him without providing any clue as to what may lie concealed within. In this passageway lies the promise of new experiences and impressions. Uncertainty and mystery accompany the visitor on this path, whose course he cannot foresee and whose end he cannot discern. Nor will he be able to predict how long he will stay there. What is certain, however, is that during his exploration he will be left to his own devices.

"The sequence of looking involves navigating space and time as a compositional factor inherent in the act of seeing and experiencing the sculpture. The passage through a piece, which can be both physical and mental, takes account of these temporal factors."[1]

II.

From Cristina Iglesias' earlier works we are familiar with similar grid like structures made from various materials, whose multifaceted arabesques are reminiscent of the Moorish palaces of the Alhambra, and whose fragmentary texts speak to us like hieroglyphs. One of the remarkable characteristics of her work is the way in which certain motifs concerning form and content evolve in a gentle flow of continuous development.

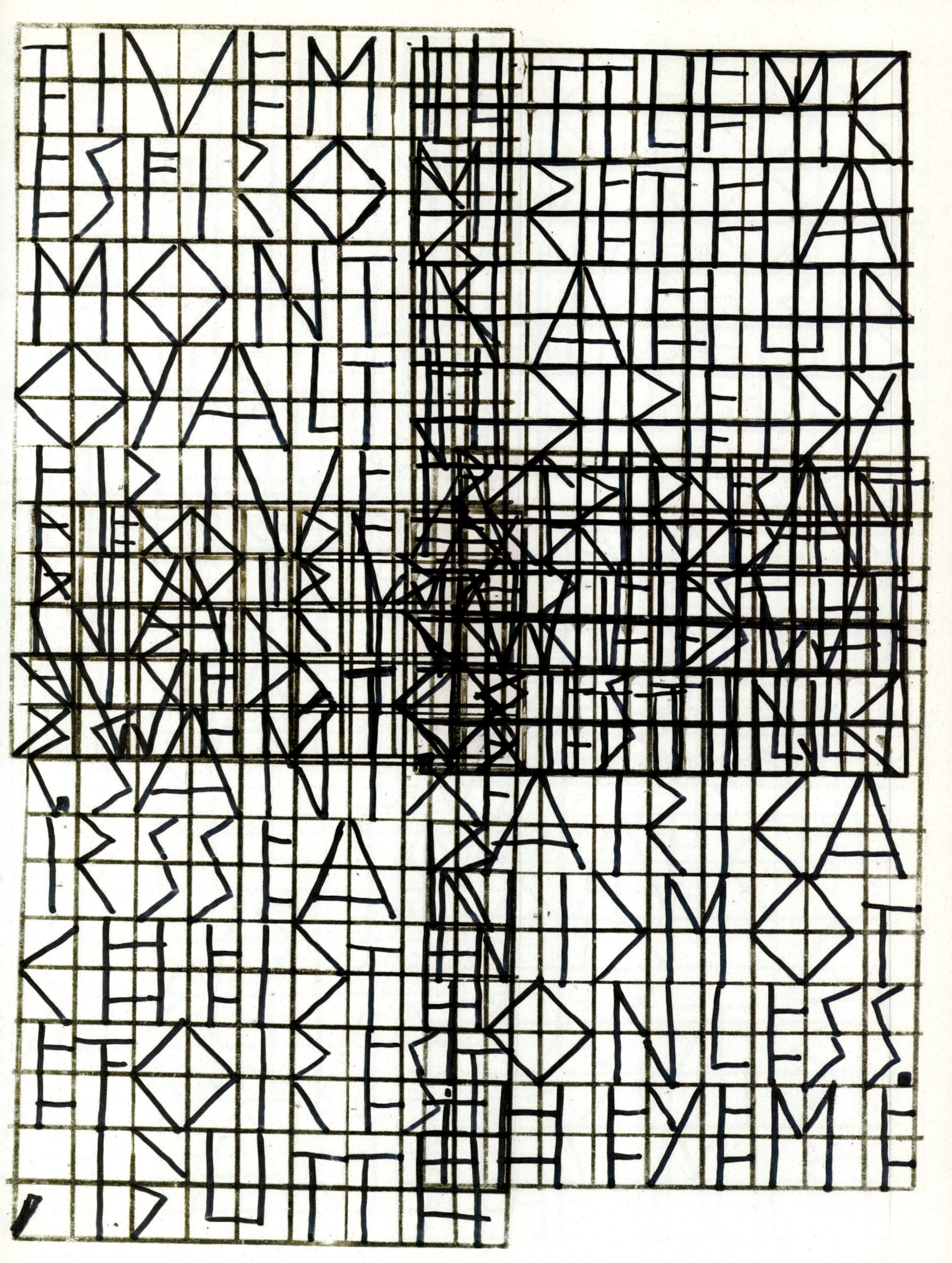

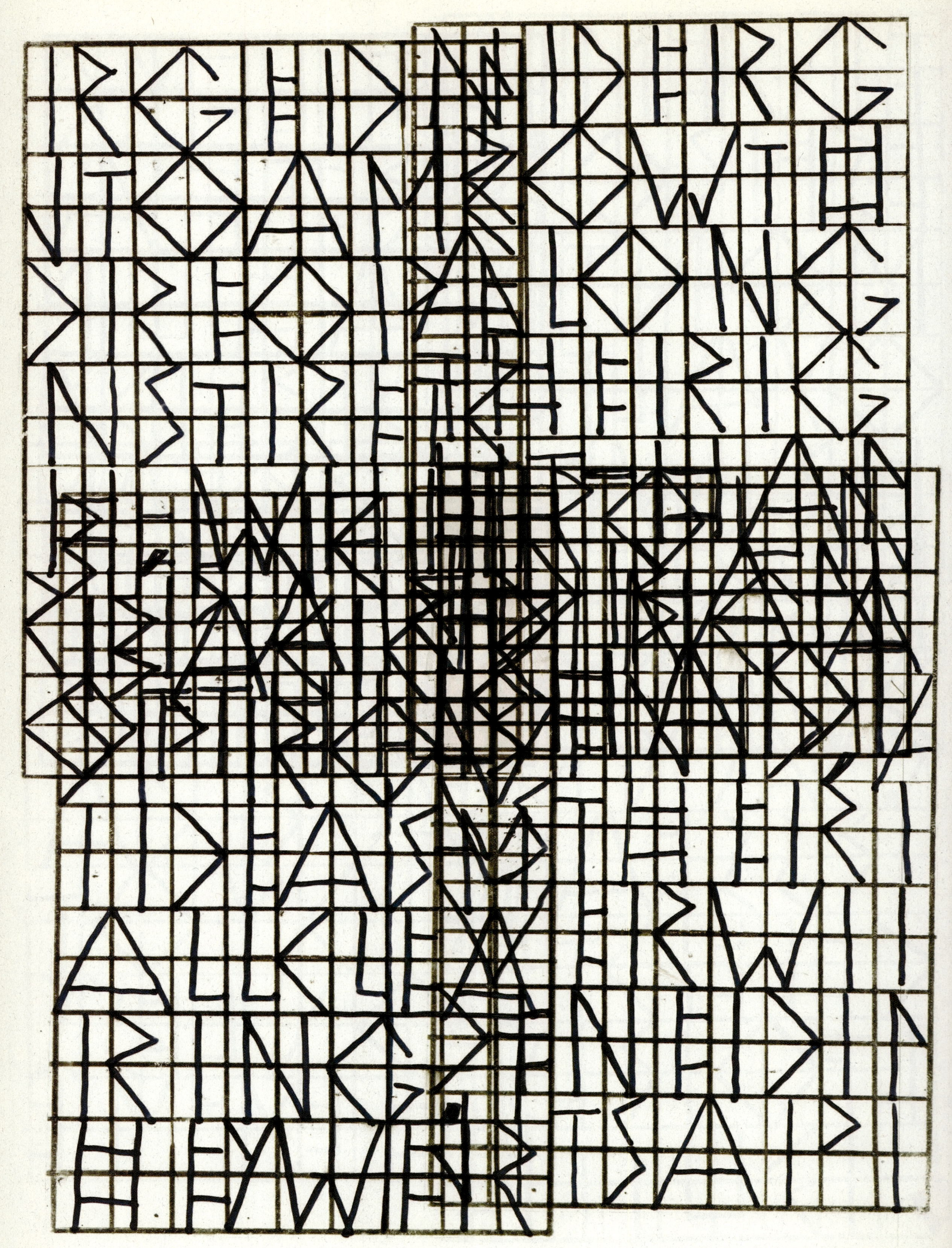

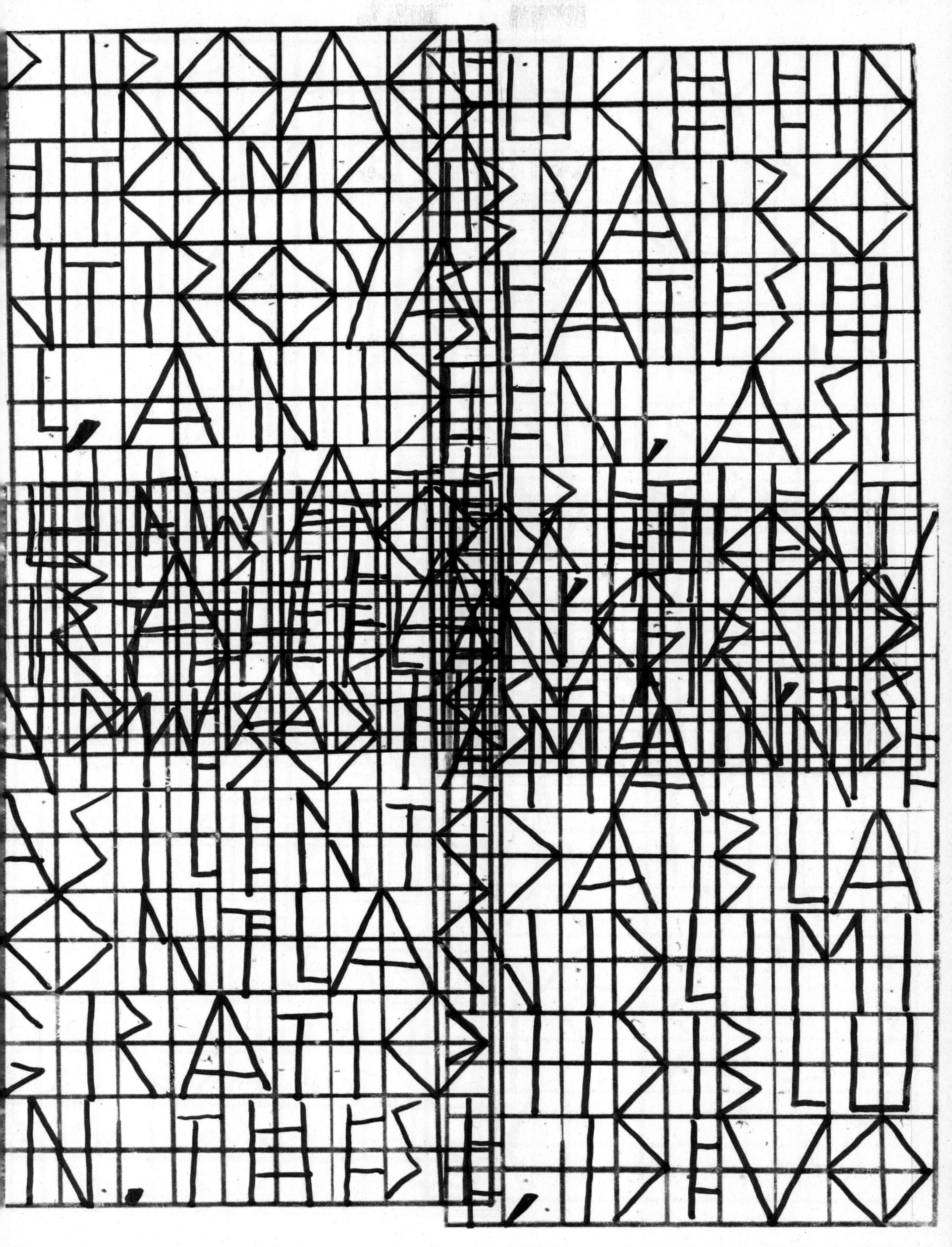

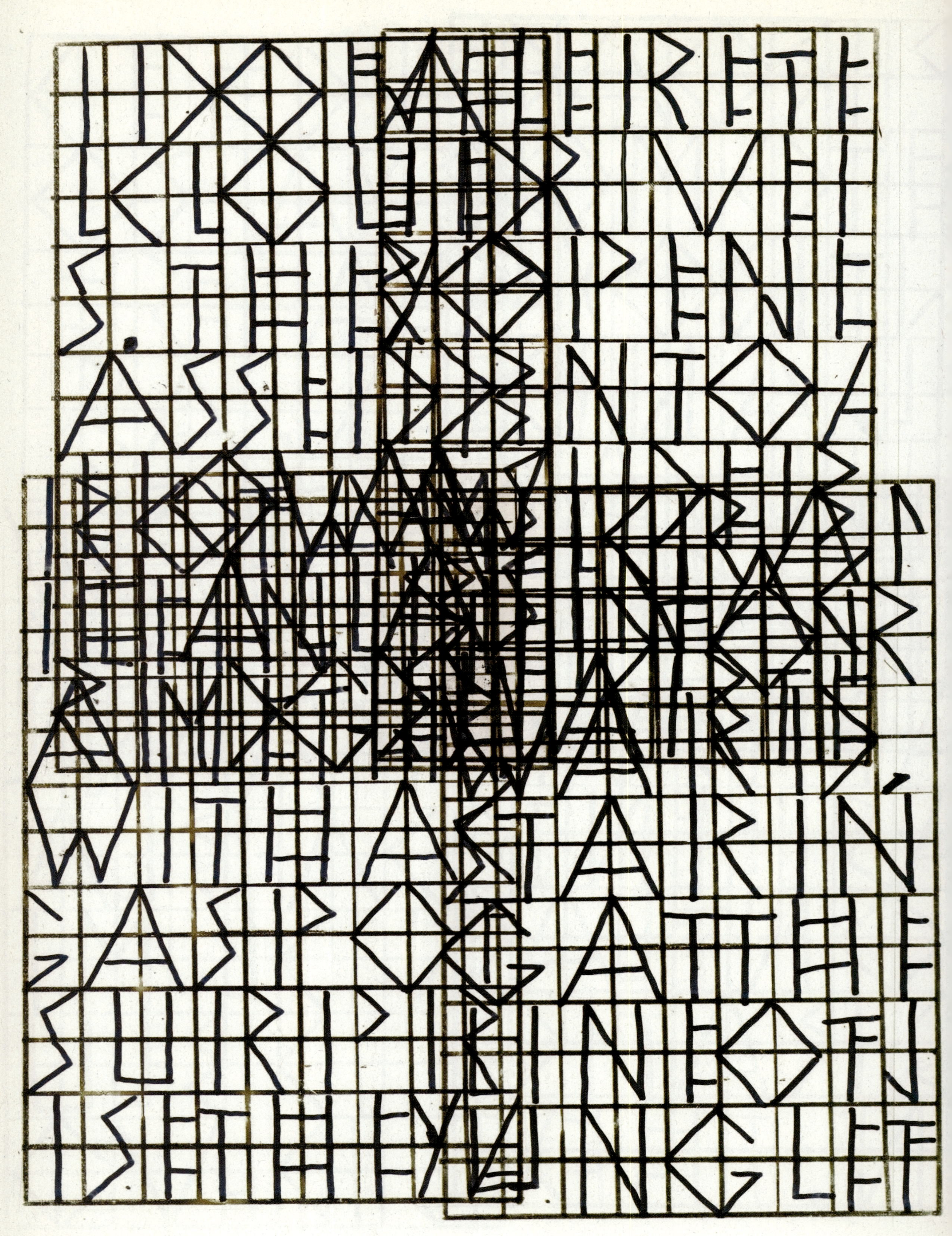

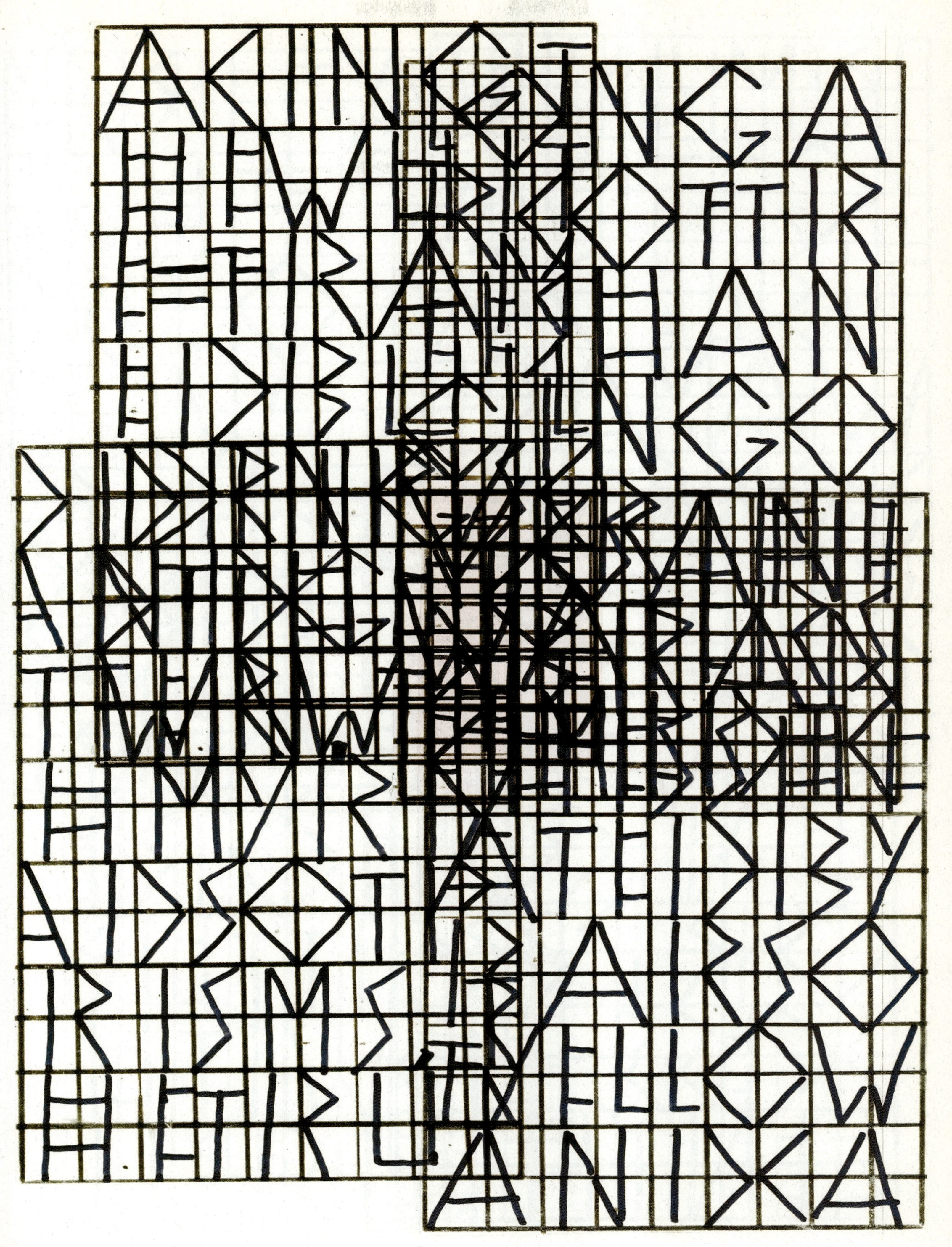

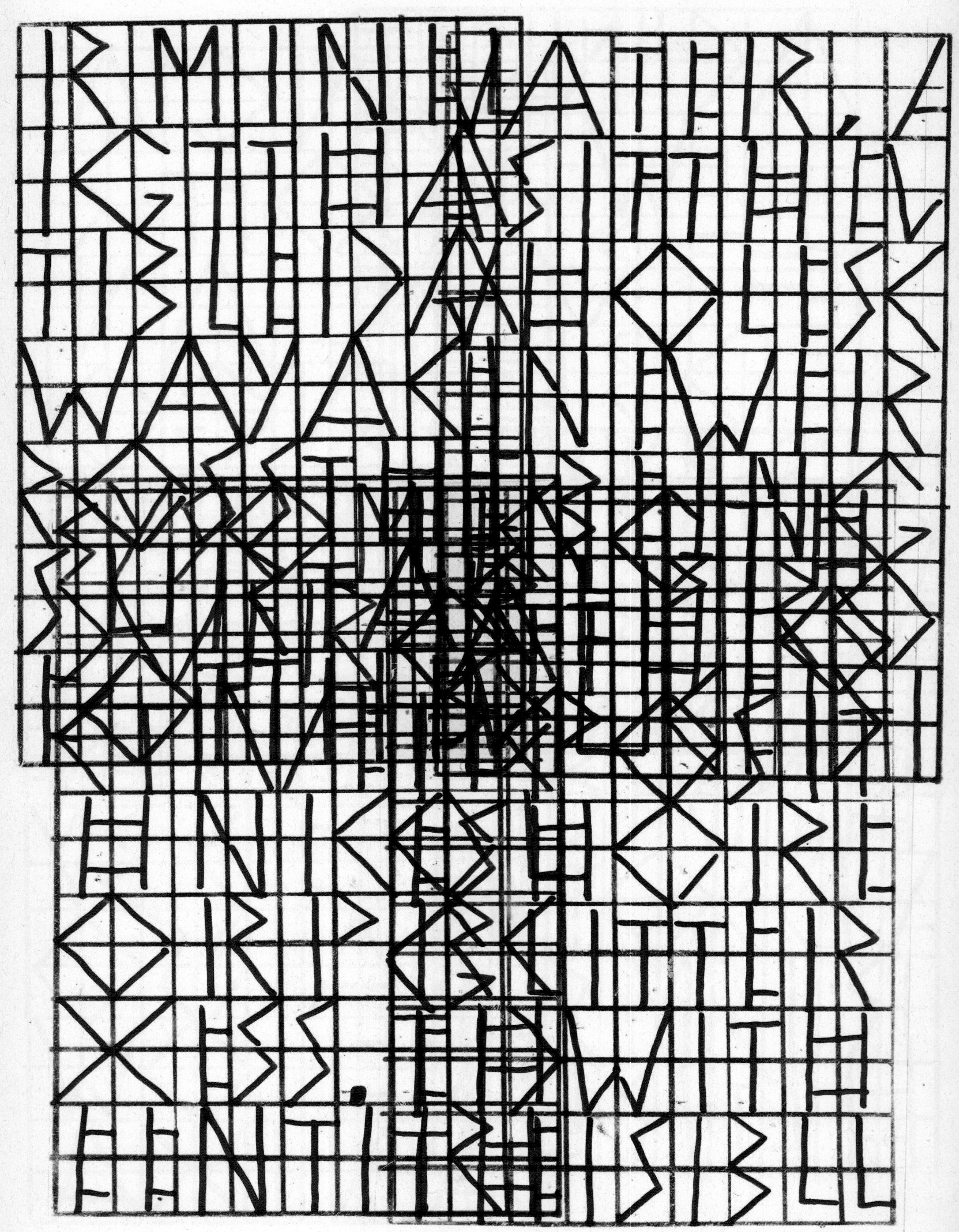

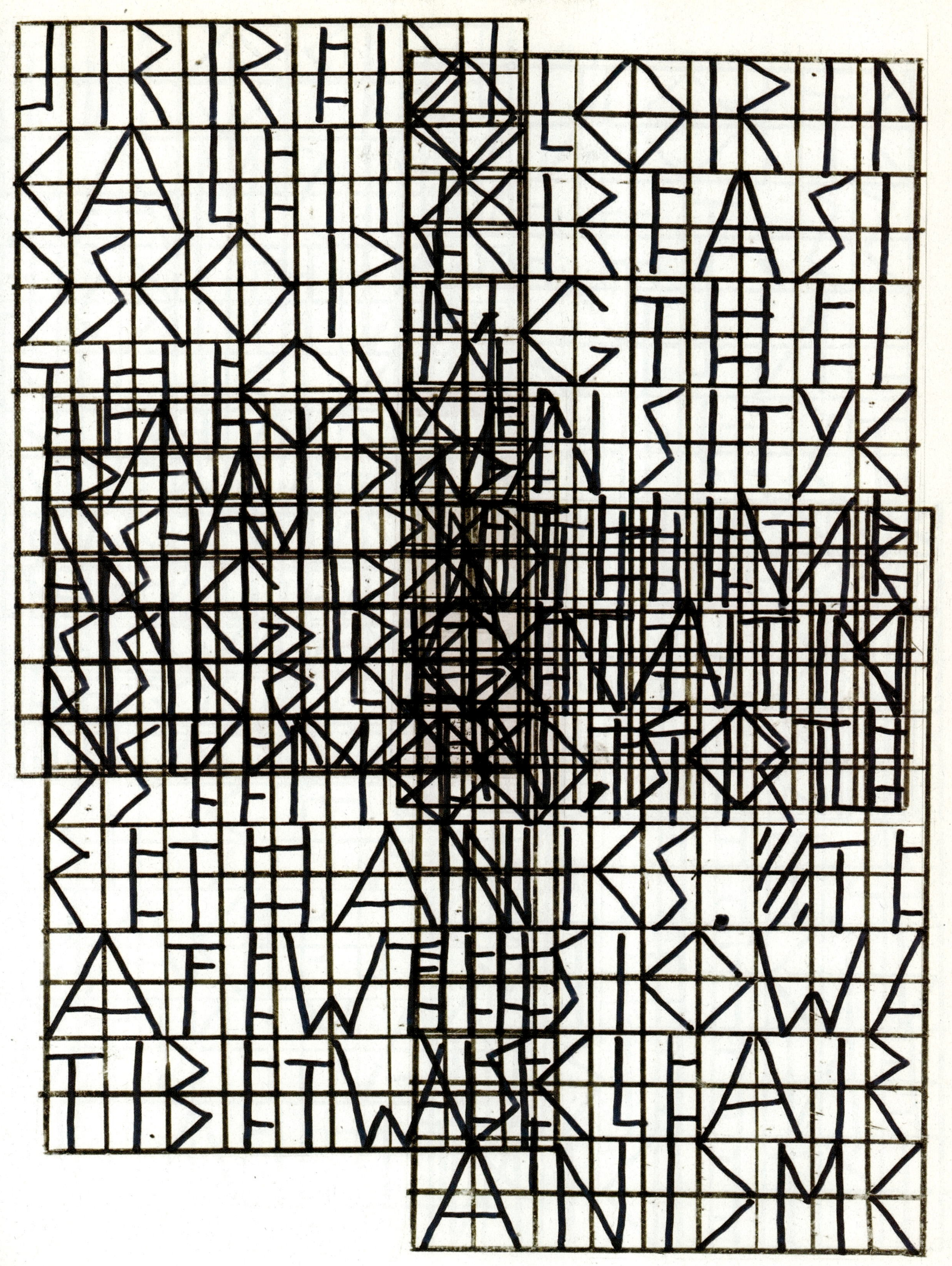

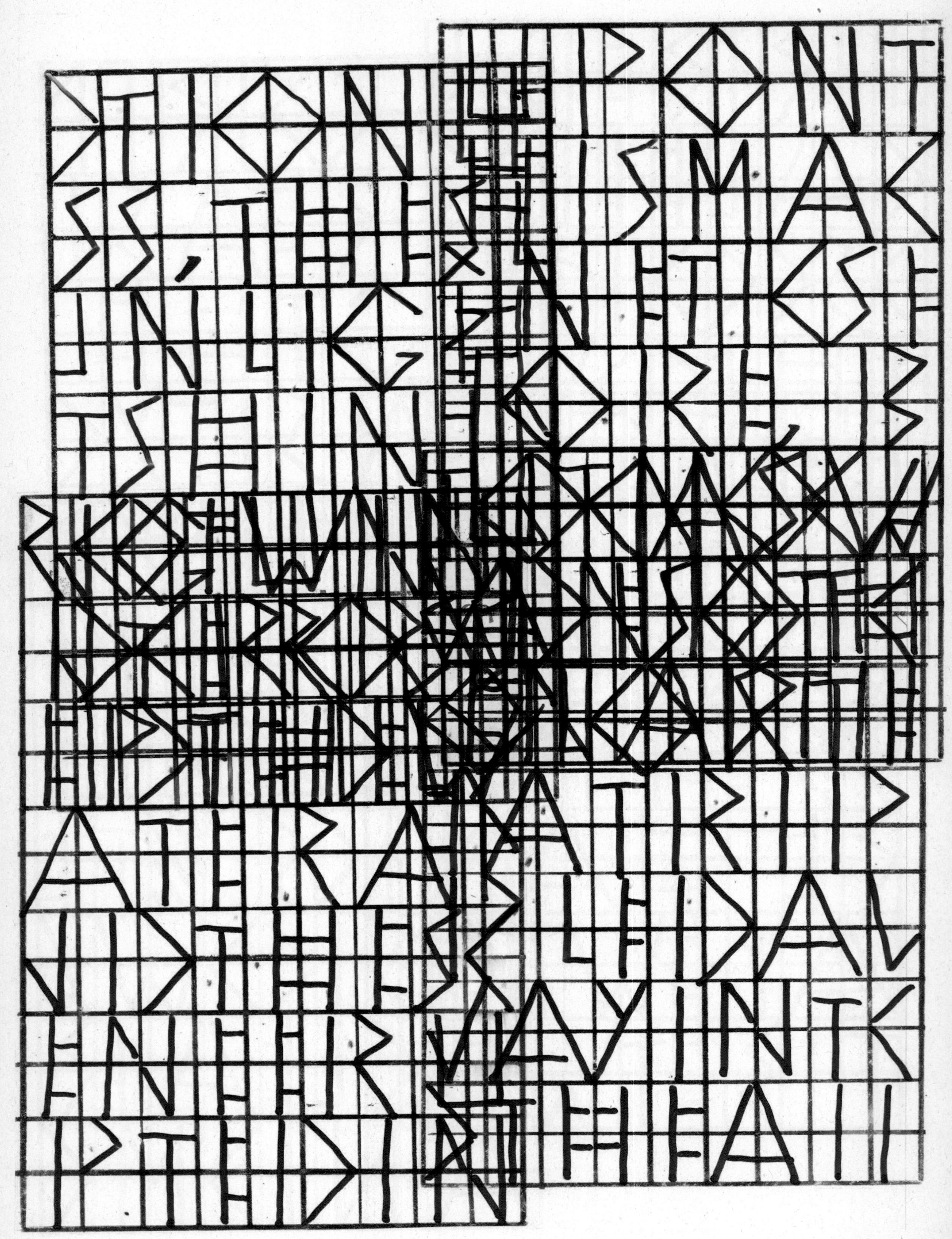

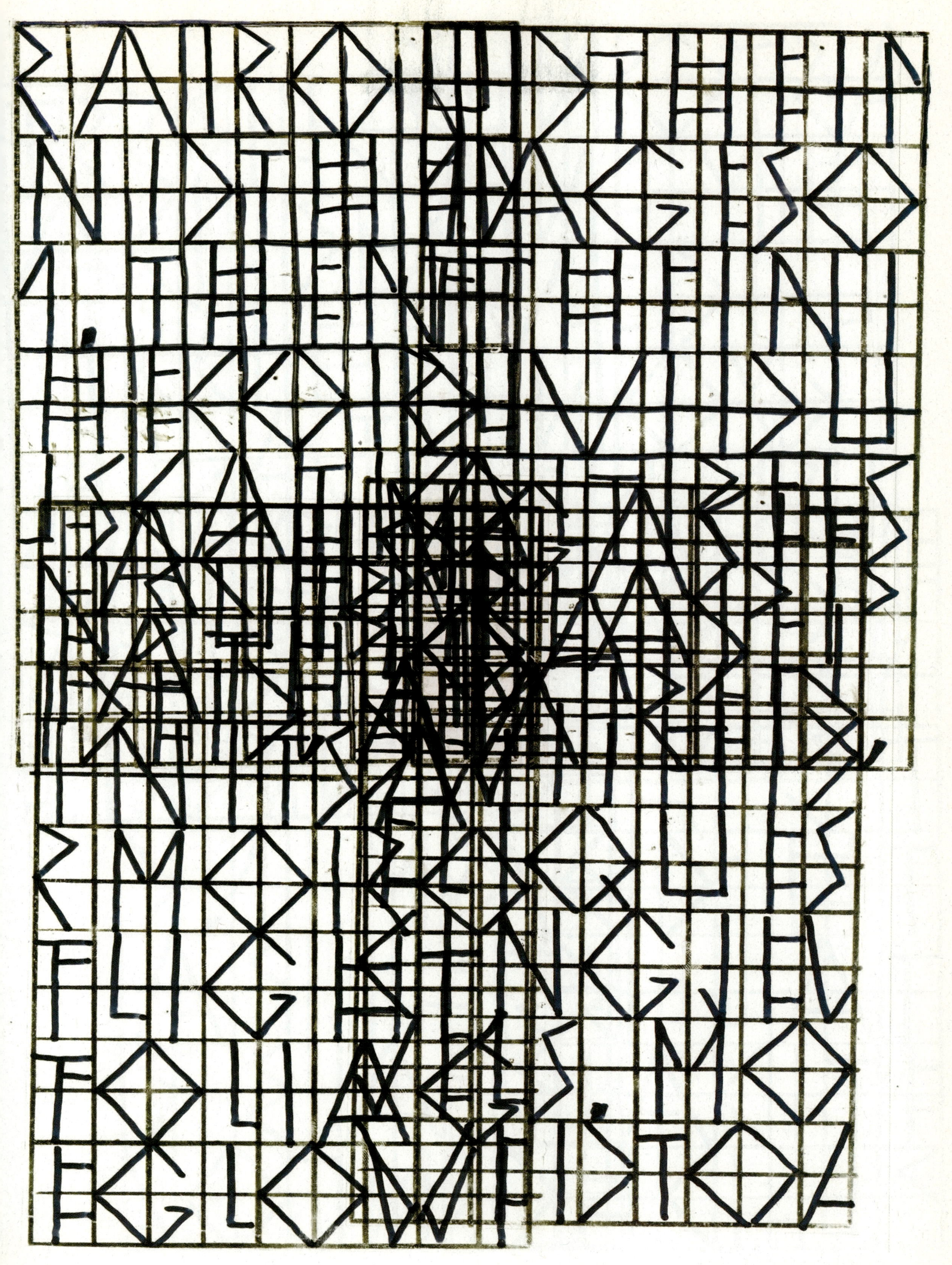

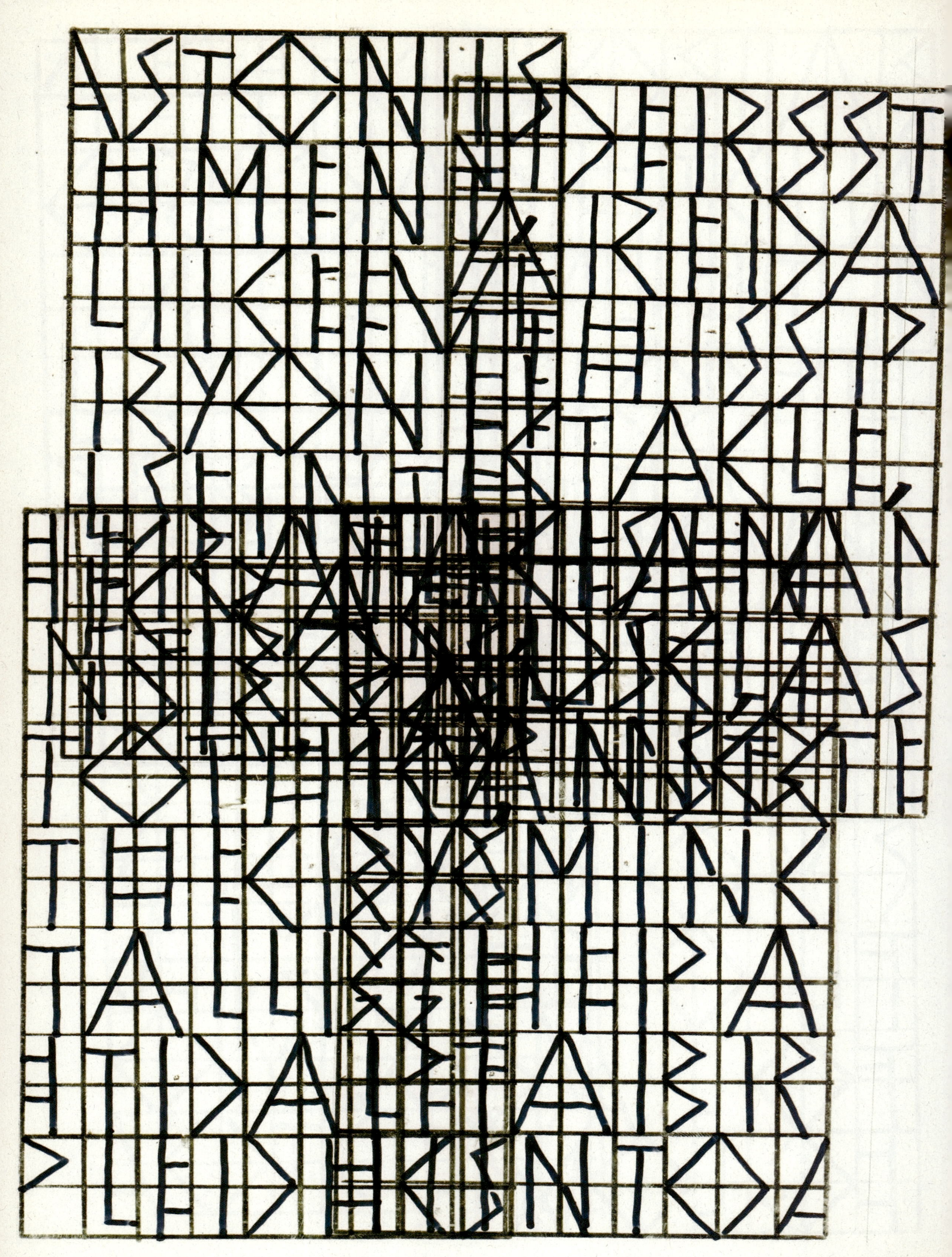

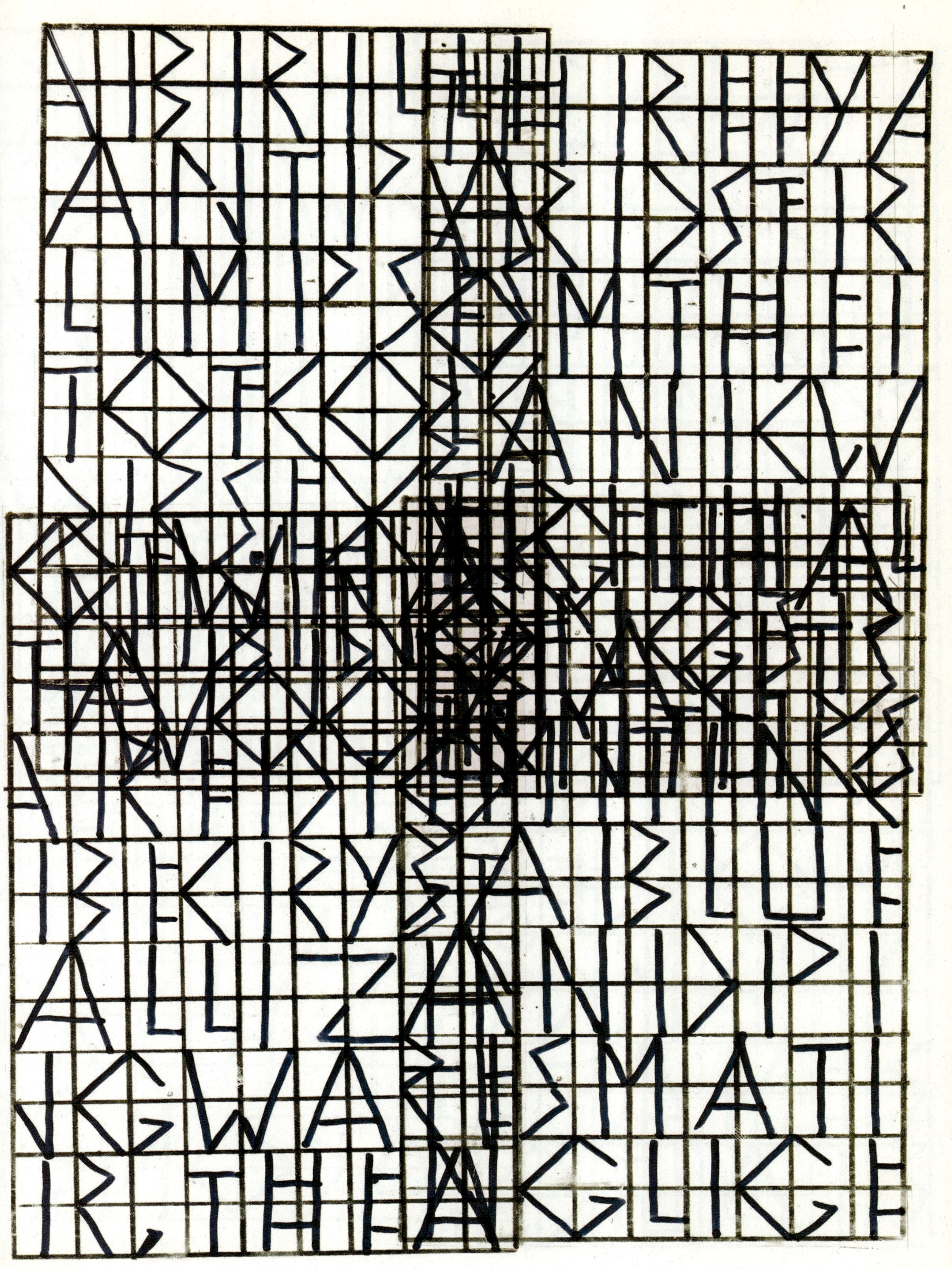

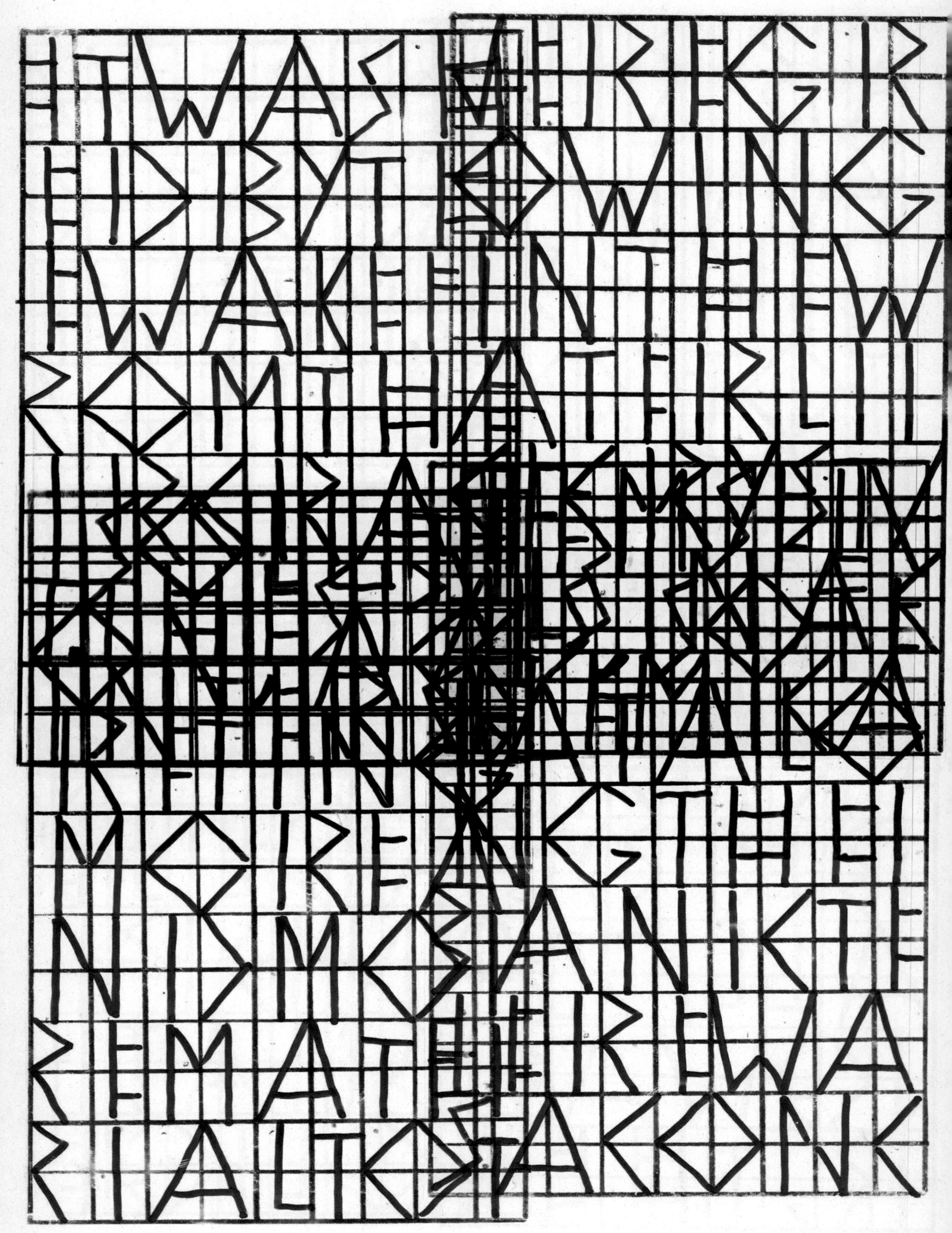

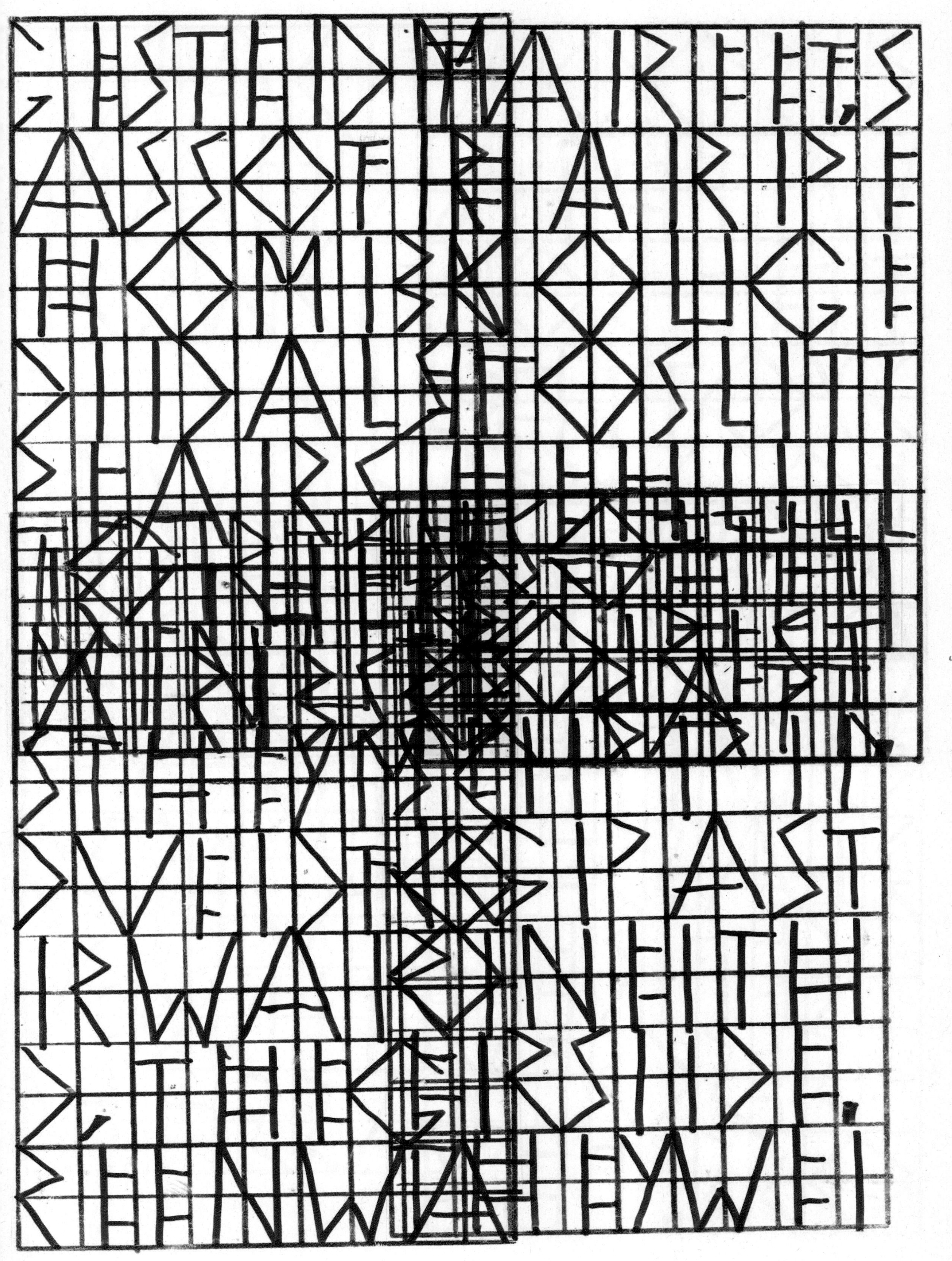

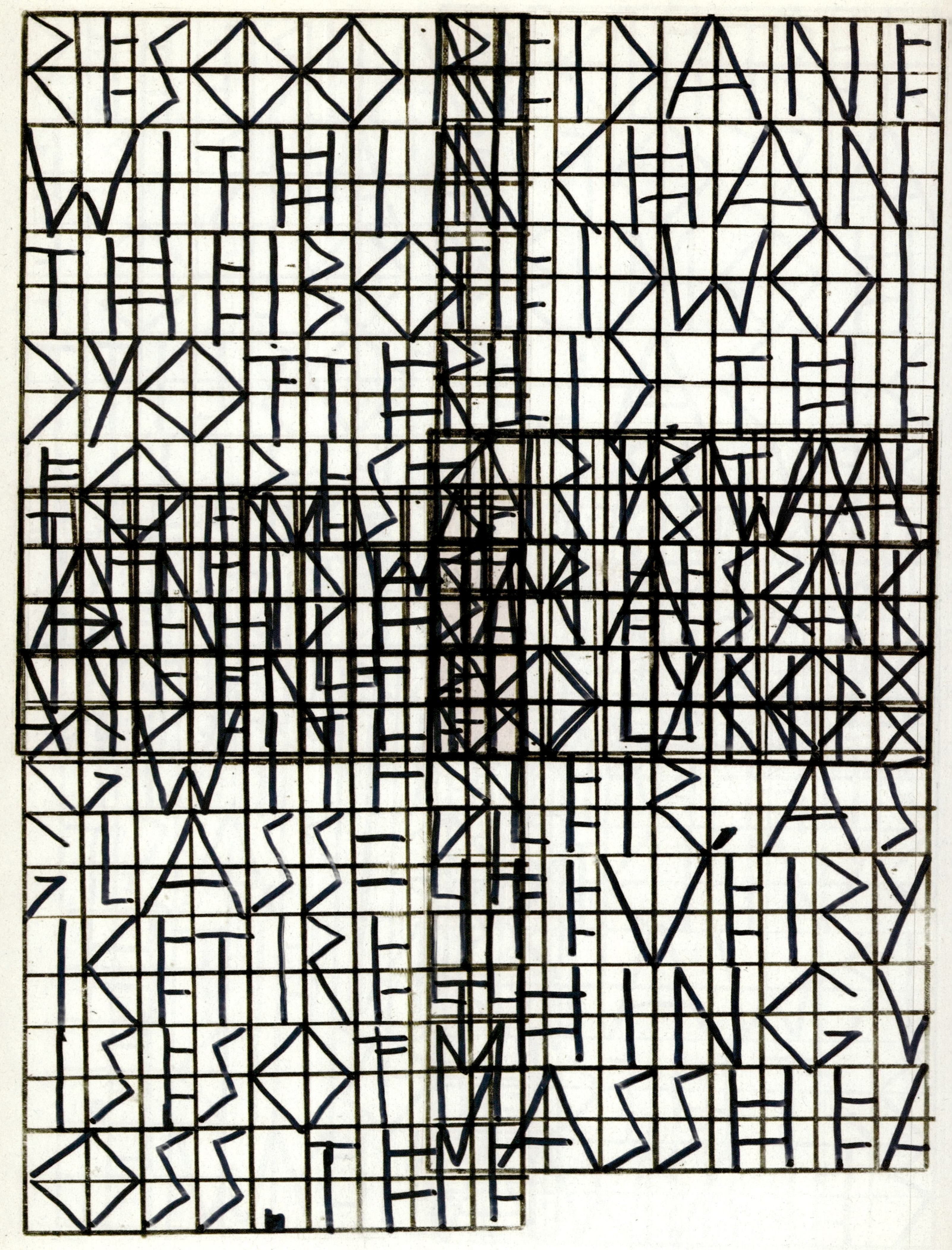

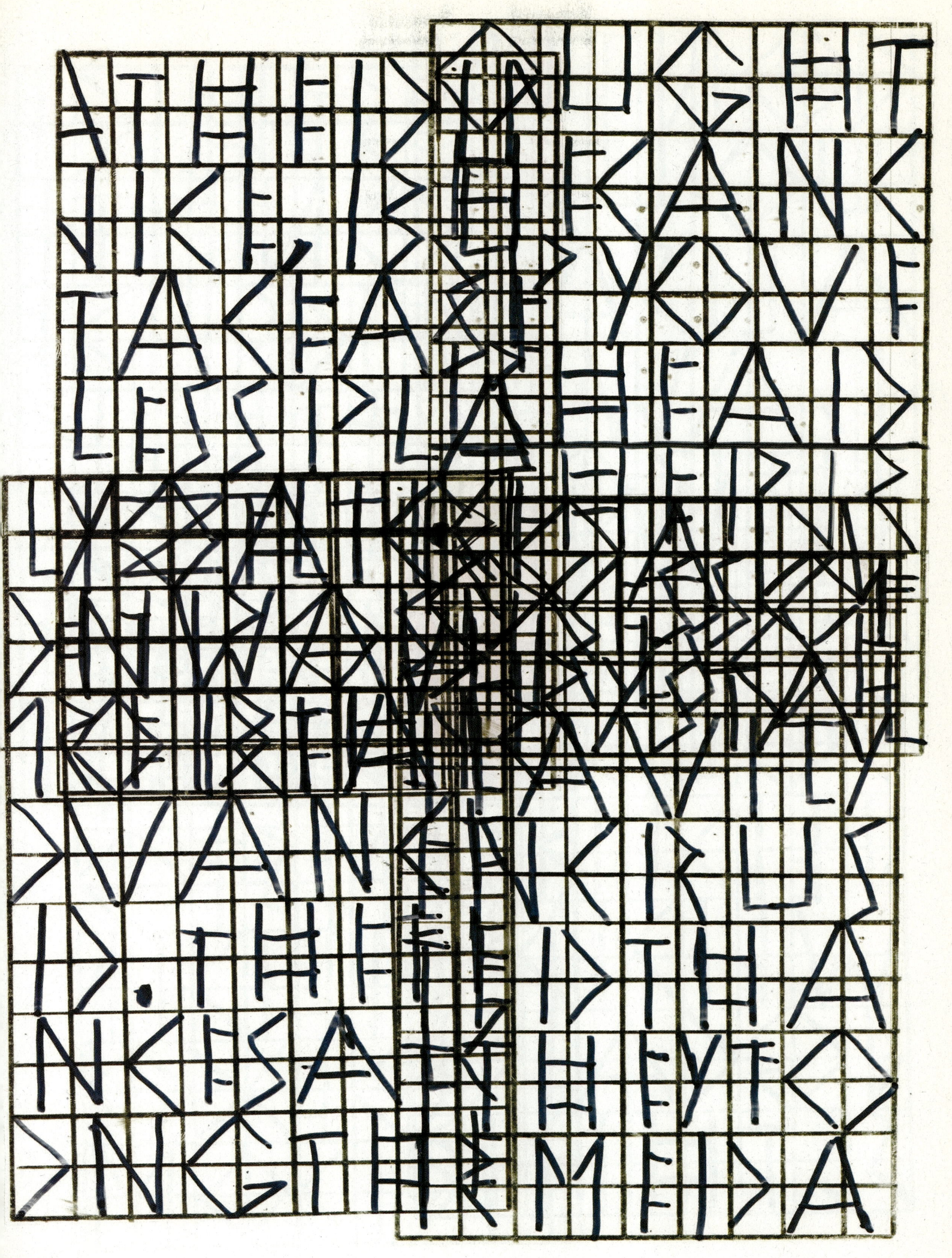

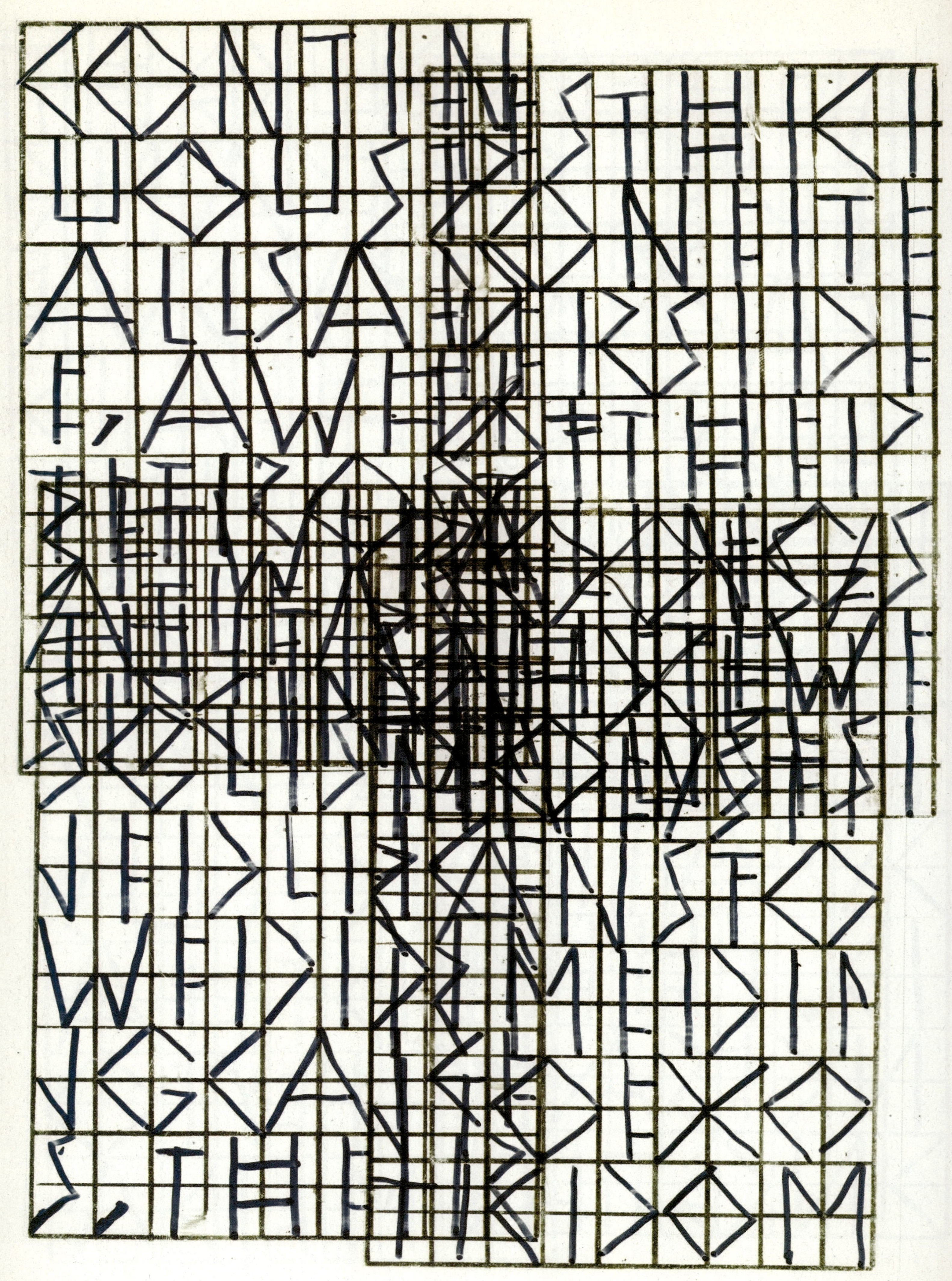

The *Corridors* combine elements of two groups of works. On the one hand the artist returns to her *Celosias/Jalousies* (1996/97), filigree cabinets made up of nested latticework. She has been creating these since the end of the nineties using wood and synthetic resin patinated with bronze powder. Their title refers to the structure of Arabic window grilles, which allow the person inside to see the world outside, but obstruct any attempt to look into the room the other way round. At the same time their title alludes to the extended meaning of the word celosia, which in Spanish can also stand for jealousy. On the other hand, the *Corridors* refer to the more recent *Pasajes/Passages* (from 2002 onwards). There the mats are of a similar structure but are made from esparto, a natural fibre similar to bast, used in Southern Europe and North Africa for various objects of everyday use. Amongst others, it is employed for weaving the kind of canopies found in Arabic bazaars as protection from the intense sun, there, as here, producing a scintillating interplay of light and shade.

Some time ago, while still working on the concept Iglesias already provided a specific description of the emerging work, calling it a variation building upon its precursors *Jalousies* and *Passages*. In this description she declares that the mats suspended from the ceiling "create a passage [...] that ends somewhere in a white room". At the same time she emphasises the function of the light which "illuminates the piece from above, throwing shadows of texts on the ground". Therefore whilst the visitor walks through the covered passageway "the shadows of the texts fall at our feet; we are above and beneath the work at the same time. If we look up, the canopy is simultaneously transparent and dense with words, presenting a vision that has nothing to do with sculpture."[2]

Iglesias makes it clear that the plastic shape of the *Corridors* can only be grasped by means of polyperspective perception of space, object and lettering. As a result, the layout of the installation on the one hand, and the literary references on the other, move into the visitors' focus.

III.

The *Corridors* installation consists of three segments encroaching upon the room. After the visitor has traversed the first of them, he finds himself roughly at the centre of the arrangement from where two more segments, of similar make but different layout, can be reached. It is in this central place that we gain an impression of the external shape of the installation and its position within the surrounding space. The zones enclosed by the elements of the installation can be experienced as a representation of the spatial alternation between interior and exterior. Instead of merely defining negatively enclosed space, however, they create spaces which are located outside the set passageways. The visitor will consequently experience the entire installation as an analogy to an urban landscape, its labyrinthine disorientation arising from occupied and vacant spaces. "I am interested in that serendipitous imposition that [...] conditions the urban landscape. To use it like a system of signs that you can decipher like hieroglyphics. Codes that require time and attention to be deciphered. There is never a decorative intention in the use of these signs; rather there is a manipulation of those mechanisms of construction and ornamentation to construct a place of representation."[3]

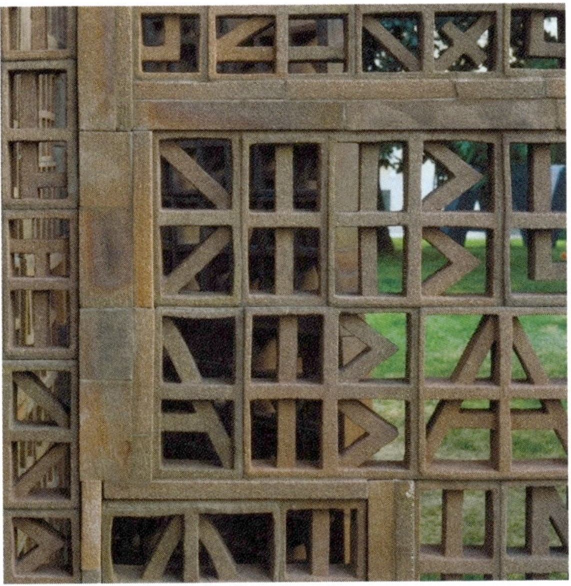

Untitled (Celosía IX), 2005. Clay, 560 x 480 cm, Collection Plácido Arango (Foto: Luis Asin)

The extraordinary location of the enormous exhibition space is determined by its setting within the museum. Almost embedded in its architectonic context the approximately 300 sqm hall extends over four staggered levels and can be viewed from a lofty gallery. From there the visitors can gain an overview of the *Corridors*. We look through the "curtain" formed by the numerous wires from which the mats are suspended, and onto the flat "roofs", which span the entire room and show him the layout and the dimensions of the installation. This overview, in its turn, obstructs the inspection of the passageways and the visitors within, who are left to the contemplation of the inscriptions inside. Mutual eye contact is only possible outside the passageways.

But back to the centre of the installation where the *Corridors* meet. Here the visitor's apprehension, built up on the prescribed path through the installation, can ease. It slips away upon reaching a spot where we quasi find ourselves again, in so far as we recover our bearings. We discover that the labyrinthine illusion we fell for is not actually maintained. Since Antiquity the notion of the labyrinth as an architectural concept has been overpowered by its colloquial and literary interpretation, which differs from its actual nature. This creates a complex figure of movement, separating an internal space from the exterior. A single entrance leads to the only path, which, by perpetual alteration of direction, inevitably leads to the centre, where the visitor finds himself completely enclosed. Following the inherent logic of the installation, the only way out is to turn back and follow the path which previously led inside. Iglesias' installation alludes to the labyrinthine system as an intellectual construct, complicating its accessibility through integrated text fragments. This stems from the fact that the "... narration takes on a life of its own moving away from the images until we are lost. The only way to find yourself is to travel down two roads at the same time. Or, in the words of American baseball player, Yogi Berra: *When you come to a fork in the road, take it!*"[4]

In Iglesias' spatial "inventions" these imaginary spaces give the impression of citations drawn from literary sources, the origins of

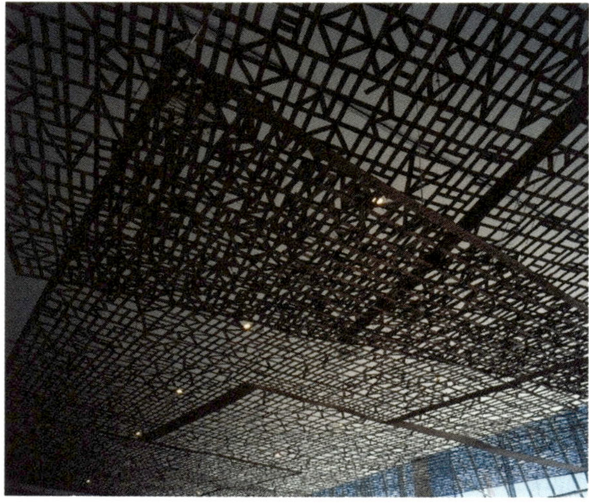

Permanent Piece for International Convention Center Barcelona, 2004. Braided wire, steel cables, 17 screens, each 1300 x 900 cm, over-all 15000 x 3000 cm
(Foto: Kristien Daem)

which the artist does not keep from the visitor. She has referred to the texts used in her interviews and they are quoted in her catalogues. Her pictorial strategy aims to produce a comparative interpretation of the different visual realities. The why and how of her use of texts from Joris-Karl Huysmans' *A Rebours* and Raymond Roussels *Impressions d'Afrique* in her earlier works has already been discussed extensively in the context of previous exhibitions. They are based upon an examination of an analogue "idea of 'invention'", which produces a space "that has never existed". Iglesias is concerned with the description of such a space "within another room", which encloses the visitor with its static components and inserted symbols. "The description of an imagined garden with touches of both real, lived experience and the purest fantasy. In the lattices the reconstruction of the text is part of the work and at the same time presents an impossibility. The fragmentation of the text imposes an extended, expanded time that is difficult to follow or even endure. This would occur if we were shut up in a room with hieroglyphics all over the walls. My intention is not so much to enclose as to surround. There is a whole idea of mapping inside those pieces that requires a strategy of movement. Like when you are lost."[5]

IV.

Once the visitors have discovered the writing they are no longer simply moving in a sculptural work, but simultaneously, and even more so, in an space both inscribed and descriptive. The integration of static framework and fleeting meaning adheres to a formal strategy which intensifies the sculptural form in its striving for autonomy with the help of pictorial fragments. Their "texture" appears here, in a literal interpretation of the Latin meaning of the word, as an "ornate fabric" which isolates the visitors in an unexplored space. The riddles it poses cannot be solved solely from a worldly point of view but challenge the visitor to exercise a high degree of otherworldly imagination. They become almost impalpable in the presence of the irregular boundaries of the latticework due to the simultaneous incomprehensibility of the fragmented writing. Which is to say that the concept of the sculptural work has an inherent dialectic of closed form and open interpretation, perceived as both real and fictitious at the same time. Whoever enters this space is transported out of the temporal linearity of past, present and future.

The *Corridors* represent a further stage of development of the *Pavilions* (2005). They use the same rectangular mats made of metal tracery, once again suspended from the ceiling of the exhibition space. Their layout is rectangular and the set-up is reminiscent of the effortlessness of Japanese houses – an allusion which, in its turn, contains the notion of a highly specific system of pictorial symbols. Nonetheless they convey a static principle of locational fixation which links them to the *Jalousies* and which, despite their transparency, conveys a feeling of being enclosed.

The literary frame of reference is Arthur C. Clarke's 1973 science fiction novel *Rendezvous with Rama*. It deals with the classic theme of the genre, the first encounter between man and extraterrestrial intelligence. Here it is manifest in the encounter with a gigantic spacecraft of mysterious origin, traversing our galaxy with an unknown destination. The crew of the space ship have only a few days to examine the craft registered as number 31/439 under the code-name "Rama". Its investigation confirms the impression they gained from afar – it is a perfect, cylindrical shape with a length of 50 kilometres. When the crew lands on it and enters the craft, they find themselves in a bizarre world with the appearance of a surreal technical work of art. The further the astronauts and scientists intrude into this fascinating artificial space, the more they are seized by its wondrous appearance which seems to pose more questions than it answers. With *Rama* Clarke created a myth which almost took on a life of its own. The leading role in it is reserved not for the heroic intruders, but for the target of their adventurous mission, this unbelievable spacecraft and its autarkic world.

Iglesias is, without question, not concerned with the literal translation of Clarke's utopian vision into a sculptural language. The latter's literary invention of an inanimate extraterrestrial world is sheer fantasy, its true nature remaining hidden. Rama is a microcosm overwhelming due to its sheer scope and diversity. Its artificial celestial body displays a superhuman inner perfection. Yet at the same time it conveys the impression of isolation and emptiness. Its fantastic

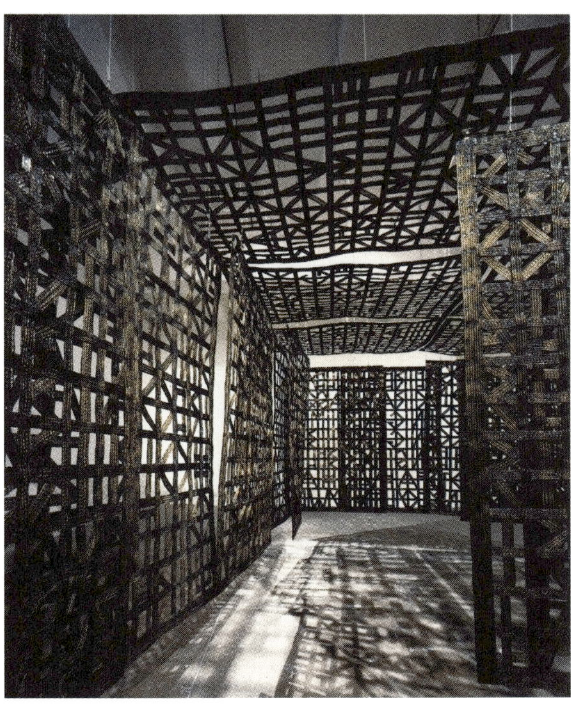

Pavilion I and II Suspended in a Room, 2005. Braided wire, steel cables, 50 screens, each 185 x 120 cm, Pavilion I, Tate Gallery, London (Foto: Attilio Maranzano)

landscapes also include an extensive region wich resembles a chessboard whose individual fields are occupied with items of the most diverse shape, structure and material. They seem to the intruder like the Ramanian "Museum of Fine Arts", in which he discovers, amongst other things, phenomena like "carpets of plaited wire" and "tent-like constructions made from barbed wire resembling large birdcages"[6]. It was this description of abstract concepts of form, limited only by the imagination, in which the artist has found herself.

V.

The most significant change in the *Three Suspended Corridors* lies in the dynamisation of their installation. Its spatial dimensions prise open the hermetic isolation of the *Pavilions* in favour of a state of being enclosed, which imposes an orientation towards a goal. In this sense they are constructions involving sculptural, architectonic and literary motifs and symbols, which can be deduced from the interpretation of a labyrinthine figure of motion. However, the spatial disposition of the three *Corridors* does not refer directly to the formal principles of a labyrinth. Rather, as a fiction, it seems to overlay the gestalt, to cover it in a imaginary veil. In the mythological and literary tradition the labyrinth is mostly portrayed as a tempting trap, a place where whoever enters loses himself and eventually perishes. This is above all determined by the isolated visitor's terrifying notion of what he might find at the end of the path, at the unknown place. What he will ultimately encounter is a void which throws him back upon himself in the knowledge of his mortality.

The three components of the installation each include a coherent text passage whose sentences and sentence-fragments are embedded in the mats in a coherent sequence. They are taken from J.G. Ballard's fantasy novel *Crystal World*. In it Ballard describes the threat posed to an African jungle region by a mysterious process of crystallisation, which brings on the death of both organic and inorganic matter, fixing it all in a wondrous state of torpor. From their core they emit a bizarre glow which irradi-

20

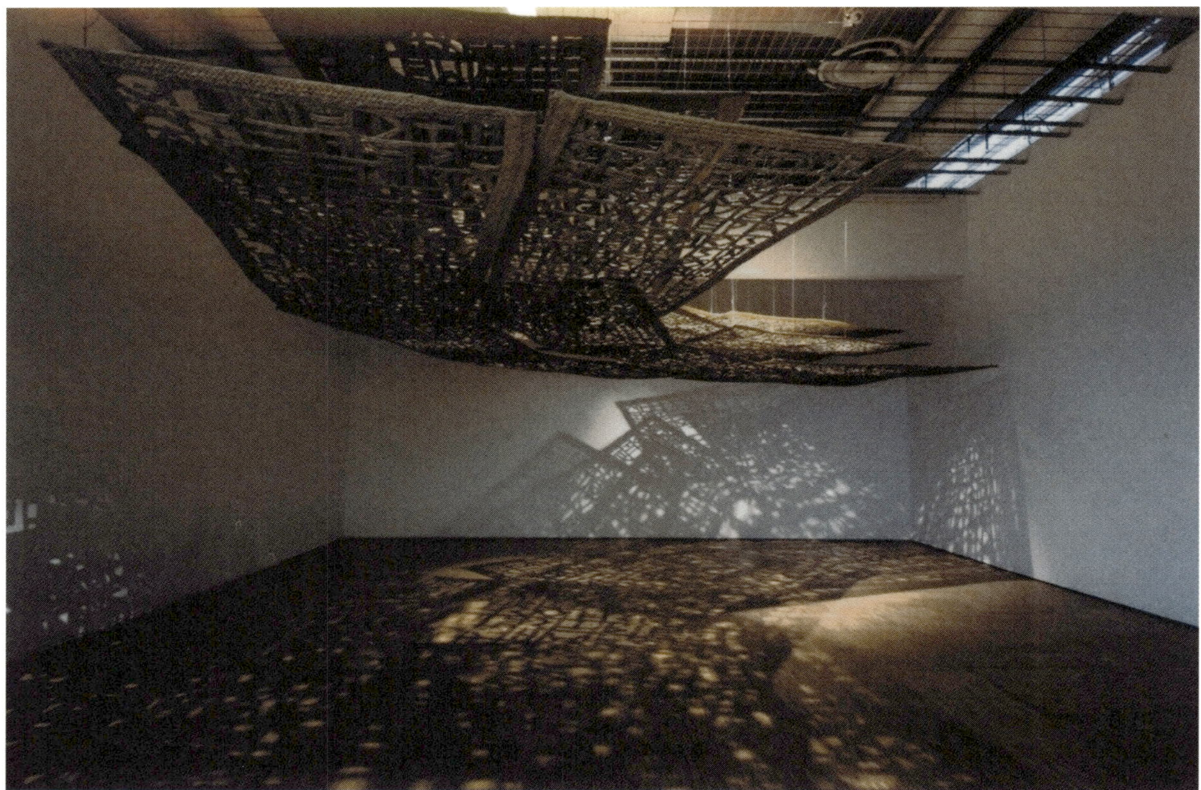

Untitled (Passage II), 2002. Raffia, 300 x 125 cm, Centre Georges Pompidou, Paris (Foto: Georges Méguerdichian)

ates the darkness of the tropical rainforest. The fascinating beauty of this bizarre transformation has a suggestive attraction, which the novel's protagonists are neither able nor willing to withstand.

Once again Iglesias restricts her "reading " to the description of the artificial phenomena of the place, the appearance of an environment transformed by crystallisation and prismatic light. She ignores the narrative and uses the description of the actualities. Neither the people and their fateful relationships, nor the course of the action is of any interest to her. The artist only filters those fragments of text which provide the setting for the scenario. The clear simplicity of the description of these supernatural events is characteristic of Ballard's narrative style. It makes this one of the most outstanding and memorable passages of the novel whose symbolism, over and above the narrative, is adopted by Iglesias. The path to the area affected by the crystallisation process leads over a river enclosed by "the high walls of the jungle" which curve in a "long arch of trees" over the surface of the water. Like in a "blurred kaleidoscope" it reflects the "overlapping bands of colour" of a vegetation"encrusted by the translucent lattice". It is an enchanted place, traversed by a road which had become "a tunnel of yellow and crimson light formed by the forest canopy overhead" and whose "crystal floor" seemed to consist of "spurs of basalt"[7]. In Ballard's *The Crystal World*, the protagonists enter an unreal zone in which time has come to a standstill and life has been frozen in miraculous petrification, where "human existence and the constant search … [have] found a dubious goal and an oppressive end"[8].

The visitors of the *Three Suspended Corridors* move in a labyrinthine passageway which surrounds us with symbols. Letters direct our attention to their symbolism of communication and negotiation. They are interwoven in the pictorial fiction, as if referring back to a distant future. Due to their descriptive nature, the effect is a state where a space extends behind the visitor's discerning eye, occupying him as much as the visible reality in front of him. We "want to see through the grating, but are being kept out of the picture, of which … [we] have already be-

come a component". Because of this we only perceive what we carry within ourselves. For a moment we are suspended in the position an archaeologist who investigates gravesites of a culture that became extinct in times long past, in order to understand …! We, however, have embarked upon a totally different kind of journey through time. Whilst he transfers the space-time context from the present to the past, the *Corridors* visitor moves in a time warp where the present extends indefinitely. Hereby the artist wants to convince us that we only have to try long enough to, sooner or later, be able to decipher and interpret the hieroglyphic signs. To use Iglesias' own words, she creates an "illusion on the threshold to reality", which the visitor briefly believes to be real. This "minute, very first moment of deception" is the point of departure from which " the journey [… into an inner labyrinth …] commences" – both for the artist and for the visitor, who experiences the presence of the installation as a dramatisation of space. Within it the *Corridors* function as antennae for the reception of "correspondences, references, integration and reflections", with whose help we rediscover the truth about ourselves[9].

Notes

1 Cristina Iglesias, interview with Gloria Moure, in: *Cristina Iglesias*, ed. by Iwona Blazwick, catalogue Museu Serralves, Porto; Whitechapel Art Gallery, London; Irish Museum of Modern Art, Dublin; Ediciones Poligrafa, Barcelona 2002, p. 23.

2 ibid. p. 26.

3 ibid. p. 50.

4 Michael Tarantino, Cristina Iglesias: Between the Natural and the Artificial, in: *Cristina Iglesias*, ed. by Iwona Blazwick, p. 93/98.

5 Cristina Iglesias, interview with Gloria Moure, in: *Cristina Iglesias*, ed. by Iwona Blazwick, p. 50/57.

6 Arthur C. Clarke, *Rendezvous with Rama*, Spectra Books, New York 1996.

7 J.G. Ballard, *Crystal World*, Farrar Straus Giroux, New York 1988, p. 65/85.

8 Review of J.G. Ballard, *Crystal World* by Thomas Harbach, September 18, 2005, on sf_fan.de.

9 Cristina Iglesias, interview with Doris von Drathen, in: Künstler – Kritisches Lexikon der Gegenwartskunst, Issue 59/17, München 2002, p. 14.

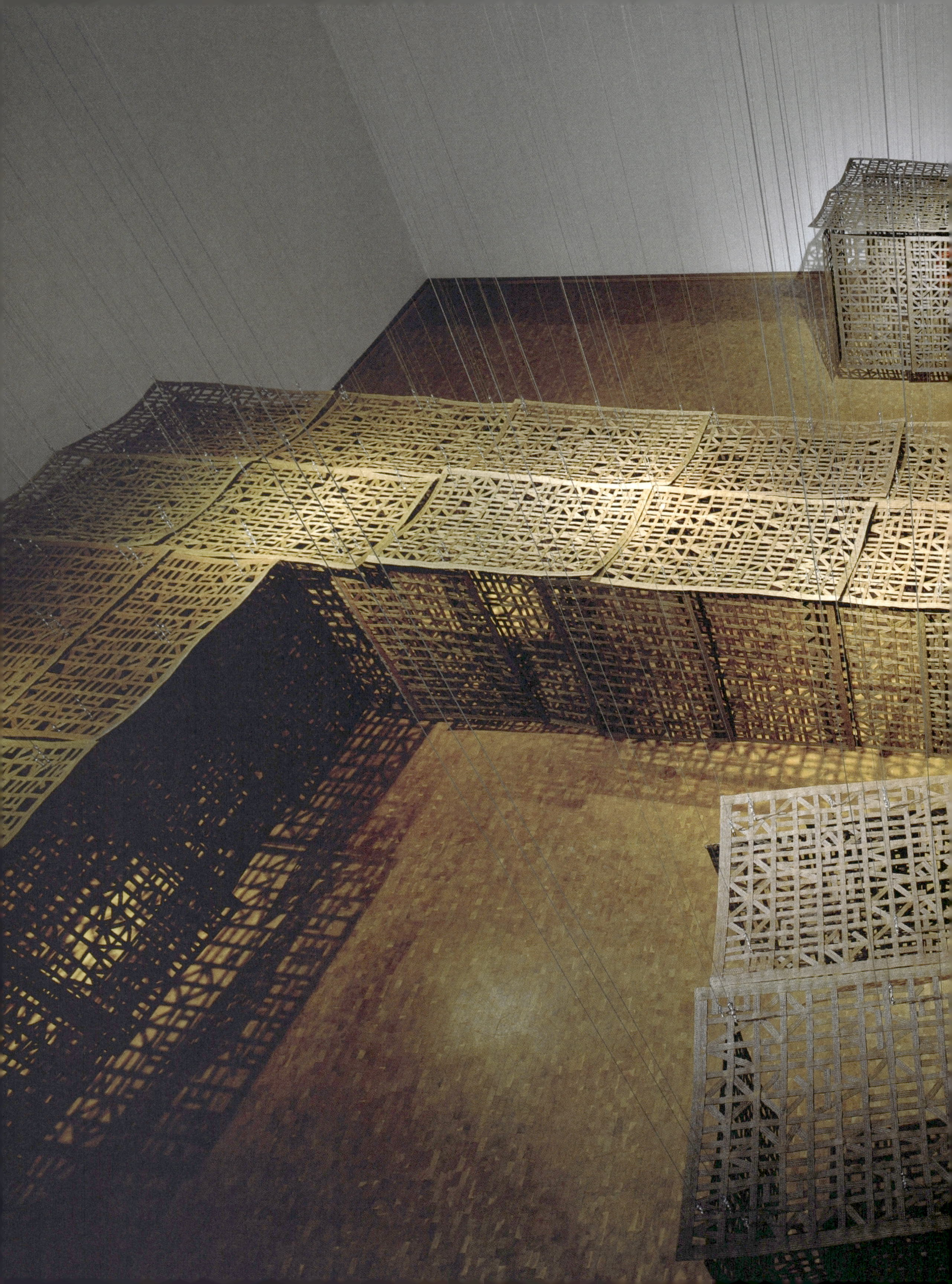

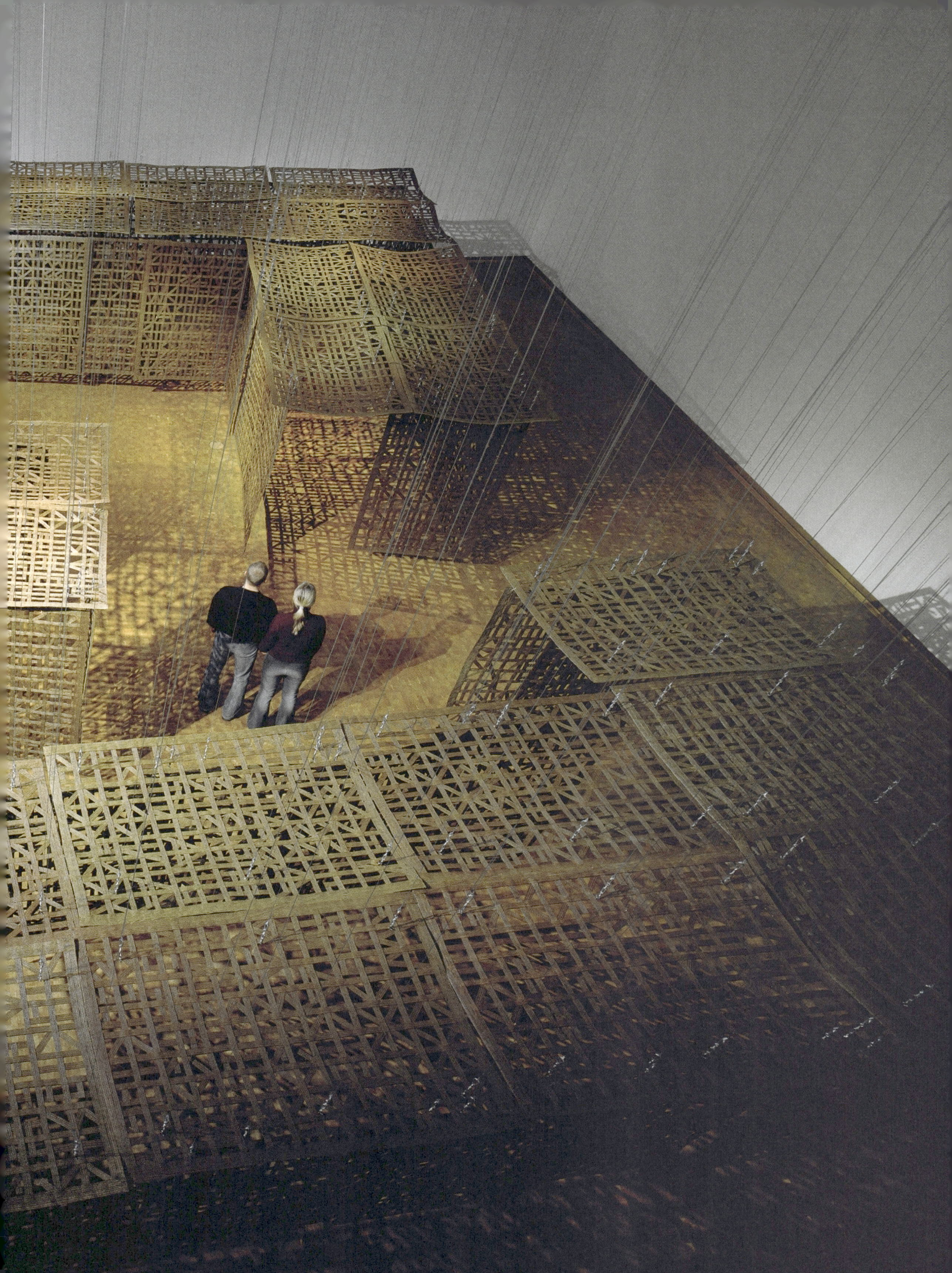

Cristina Iglesias

Biografie I Biography

Geboren | born 1956 in San Sebastian.
Lebt und arbeitet | lives and works in
Torrelodones, Madrid

**Einzelausstellungen I
Solo exhibitions**

2006 Ludwig Museum, Cologne, Germany
2005 Marian Goodman Gallery, New York
Museo Nacional Centro de Arte Reina
Sofia, Madrid, Spain
2004 Centre Convencions Internacional,
Barcelona, Spain
2003 Galerie Marian Goodman, Paris
Irish Museum of Modern Art, Dublin
Whitechapel Art Gallery, London
2002 Museu Serralves, Fundaçao Serralves,
Oporto
Bienal de Taipei, Taipei Fine Arts
Museum, Taipei, Taiwan
2001 Pepe Cobo, Sevilla
2000 Carre d'art, Museé d'art Contemporain,
Nîmes
Donald Young Gallery, Chicago
1998 Palacio de Velázquez, Museo Nacional
Centro de Arte Reina Sofia, Madrid;
Museo Guggenheim, Bilbao
A Cidade e as Estrelas, Galeria Luis
Serpa, Lisbon
Al otro lado del espejo, Sala Robayera,
Miengo, Cantabria

1997 Solomon R. Guggenheim Museum,
New York
Reinassance Society, Chicago
1996 Galerie Jean Bernier, Athens
Donald Young Gallery, Seattle
Galeria DV, San Sebastián
1994 *One Room*, Stedelijk Van Abbemuseum,
Eindhoven
Galerie Konrad Fischer, Düsseldorf
1993 Galeria Municipal de Arte ARCO,
Faro, Portugal
XIV Biennale di Venezia, Spanish
Pavilion, Venice
Mala Galerija, Moderna Galerija,
Ljubljana, Slovenia
Galerie Ghislaine Hussenot, Paris
1992 Art Gallery of York University,
North York, Ontario
1991 Kunsthalle Bern, Bern
Galerie Jean Bernier, Athens
Galerie Joost Declerq, Ghent
1990 *Cristina Iglesias/Lili Dujourie*,
Galeria Locus Solus, Genoa
Galeria Marga Paz, Madrid
De Appel Foundation, Amsterdam
Esculturas Recentes, Galería Cómicos,
Lisbon
1989 Galerie Ghislaine Hussenot, Paris
1988 Galerie Jean Bernier, Athens
Museo Bellas Artes, Málaga
Kunstverein für die Rheinlande und
Westfalen, Düsseldorf
Galerie Joost Declerq, Ghent

1987 *Sculptures: 1984–1987*, CAPC Musée
     d'Art Contemporain, Bordeaux
     Galeria Marga Paz, Madrid
     Galerie Peter Pakesch, Vienna
1986 Galeria Cómicos, Lisbon
1984 *Arqueologías*, Casa del Bocage, Setúbal
     Sequências, Galeria Cómicos, Lisbon
     Galeria Juana de Aizpuru, Madrid

**Gruppenausstellungen (Auswahl) I
(Selected) Group exhibitions**

2005 *Big Bang: Creation and Destruction*
2006 *in 20th Century Art,* Centre Georges
     Pompidou, Paris, France
     Hasta pulverizarse los ojos, BBVA/Banco
     Bilbao Vizcaya Argentaria, Bilbao, Spain
2004 *Navy Pier Walk 2004,* New York
     Horizont(e) 1984 2004, Cordoaria
     Nacional, Lisbon, Portugal
     L'Emblouissement, Galerie Nationale
     Jeu de Paume, Paris, France
     La Cuidad que Nunca Existio, Museo
     Bella Artes de Bilbao, Bilbao, Spain
2003 *Happiness: A Survival Guide for Art and
     Life,* MORI Art Museum, Tokyo, Japan
     La ciudad radiante, Fundación
     Bancaixa, II Bienal de Valencia, Valencia
     La palabra y su sombra. José Angel
     Valente: el poeta y las artes.
     Universidad Santiago de Compostela,
     Santiago de Compostela
2002 *Conversation, Recent acquisitions of the
     Van Abbemuseum,* School of Fine Arts,
     Athens, Greece
     Temper of Women, Ville de Luxembourg
     et Musée d'Histoire, Luxembourg
     *In dreams, Cristina Iglesias / Douglas
     Gordon,* Galeria Presenca, Porto,
     Portugal
2001 *Breeze of air, Hortus Conclusus,* Witte
     de With, Rotterdam
     Dialogue Ininterrompu, Musée des
     Beaux Arts, Nantes
     Atlantes, Galeria Pepe Cobo, Seville
     Group show, Donald Young Gallery,
     Chicago
     Encrucijada, Sala exposiciones de la
     Comunidad de Madrid

La Noche, Museo de Arte Contemporáneo Esteban Vicente, Segovia
2000 *Exposición Universal de Hannover 2000,*
     Spanish Pavilion, Hannover
     Enclosed and Exchanted, Museum of
     Modern Art, Oxford; Harris Museum
     and Art Gallery, Preston; Mappin Art
     Gallery, Sheffield
     *Año Mil. Año dos Mil. Dos milenios en la
     Historia de España,* Centro cultural de
     la Villa, Madrid
1999 *Damenwahl, Cristina Iglesias, Olaf
     Metzel,* Haus am Waldsee, Berlin
     North and South transcultural visions,
     Mediterranean Foundation and
     National Museum, Wroclaw, Poland
     Co-laboraciones Arquitectos- Artistas,
     Galeria Elba Benítez, Madrid; Colegio
     Arquitectos de Tenerife, Canarias; Sala
     Jorge Vieira, Lisbon
1998 Galería DV, San Sebastián
1997 *Ten years of the foundation of the
     Kunsthalle Bern,* Kunsthalle Bern, Bern
     En la piel del toro, Museo Nacional
     Centro de Arte Reina Sofia, Madrid
1995 *12 Esperientzia/Experiencias: taller de
     serigrafía, Arteleku, 1994,* Galeria
     Cruces, Madrid
     *Lili Dujourie, Pepe Espaliú, Cristina
     Iglesias,* Chisenhale Gallery, London
     Gravity's Angel, Henry Moore
     Foundation, Leeds
     Carnegie International, Museum of Art,
     Carnegie Institute, Pittsburgh
     *Andreas Gursky, Cristina Iglesias, Juan
     Muñoz, Eric Poitevin,Yvan Salomone,
     Pia Stadtbaumer, Sue Williams,* Jean
     Bernier Gallery, Athens
1994 *Bildumak/Colecciones,* Koldo Mitxelena
     Kulturunea, San Sebastián
     *Spuren von Ausstellungen der Kunst-
     halle in Zeitgenössischer Kunst,* Kunst-
     halle Bern, Bern
     Group Show, Donald Young Gallery,
     Seattle
     Artscape Norway, Moskenes, Islas
     Lofoten, Norway
     *Cristina Iglesias, Eva Lootz y Soledad
     Sevilla. La voce del genere,* Instituto
     Cervantes, Rome

1993 *Juxtaposition*, Charlottenborg, Copen-
hagen
*The sublime Void (On the Memory of
Imagination)*, Koninklijk Museum voor
Schone Kunster, Antwerp
XLV Biennale di Venezia, Spanish
Pavilion, Venice
Group Show, Donald Young Gallery,
Seattle
XIII Salón de los 16, Museo Centro de
Arte Reina Sofía, Palacio de Velázquez,
Madrid

1992 *Colección del IVAM. Adquisiciones
1985–1992*, Insituto Valenciano de Arte
Moderno, Valencia
*Los ochenta en la colección de la
Fundación "La Caixa"*, Estación Plaza de
Armas, Seville
Los últimos días/The Last days, Salas del
Arenal, Seville
Pasajes: Actualidad del Arte Español,
Exposición Universal, Spanish Pavilion,
Seville
Tropismes, Centro Cultural Tecla Sala,
Hospitalet, Barcelona
Lux Europae, Edinburgh, *Group Show*,
Donald Young Gallery, Seattle

1991 *Metropolis*, Martin-Gropius-Bau, Berlin
*Espacio mental: René Daniëls, Thierry
De Cordier, Isa Genzken, Cristina Iglesias,
Thomas Schütte, Jan Vecruysse*, Centro
del Carmen, IVAM, Valencia
*Clemente, Doren, Iglesias, Mol,
Sarmento*, Gallery Louver, New York
*Rodney Graham, Cristina Iglesias, Tony
Cragg*, Galeria Marga Paz, Madrid

1990 *The Eighth Biennale of Sydney: The
Readymade Boomerang: Certain rela-
tions in Twentieth century Art*, Art
Gallery of New South Wales, Sydney
Hacia el paisaje/Towards the landscape,
Centro Atlántico de Arte Moderno,
Las Palmas de Gran Canaria

1989 *Jeunes sculptures espagnols: au ras
du sol, le dos au mur*, Centre Albert
Borschette, Brussels
Spain Art today, Museum of Modern
Art, Takanawa
Psychological Abstraction, House of
Cyprus, Deste Art Foundation of
Contemporary Art, Athens

*Förg, Iglesias, Spaletti, Vercruysse, West,
Wool*, Galerie Joost Declerq, Ghent;
Max Hetzler Gallery, Köln; Luhring
Augustine Gallery, New York; Galerie
Peter Pakesch, Vienna; Galeria Marga
Paz, Madrid; Galleria Mario Pieroni,
Rome
*Presencia e procesos sobre as ultimas
tendencias da arte*, Casa de Parra,
Santiago de Compostela

1988 *Rosc '88: The poetry of vision*, Royal
Dublin Society, The Guinness Hop Store
and the Royal Hospital Kilmainham,
Dublin
*Three spanish artists: Cristina Iglesias,
Pello Irazu y Fernando Sinaga*, Donald
Young Gallery, Seattle
Artisti spagnoli contemporanei,
Rotonda di Via Besana and Studio
Marconi, Milan
Spanish Sculpture, Galerie Barbara
Farber, Amsterdam
Escultura, Galeria Juana de Aizpuru,
Madrid

1987 *Muur Voor Een Schilderij/Vloer voor een
sculptuur*, (project with Paul Robbretch
and Hilde Daem), De Apple Founda-
tion, Amsterdam
Beelden en Banieren, Fort Asperen
Acquoy, Holland
*Quatrièmes ateliers internationaux des
Pays de la Loire*, Fondation nationale
des Art Graphiques et Plastiques,
Abbaye royale de Fontevraud;
Manufacture des Tabacs, Nantes;
Musée d'Art et d'Archéologie de la
Roche-sur-Yon; Palais des Congrès de la
Ville du Mans; Palais des Congrès de la
Ville de Saint-Jean de Monts; Chapelle
Saint-Julien de l'Hopital; Château-
Gonthier
*Proyecto para una colección de arte
actual*, Galeria Juana de Aizpuru,
Madrid
*Espagne 87: Dynamiques et Inter-
rogations*, ARC, Museè d'Art Moderne
de la Ville, Paris
En la piel del toro, Palacio de Velázquez,
Museo Nacional Centro de Arte Reina
Sofia, Madrid

1986 *17 artistas/17 autonomías,* Pabellón
Múdejar, Seville
8 de Marzo, Antiguo Colegio de San
Agustin, Diputación Provincial, Málaga
L'attitude, Galeria Cómicos, Lisbon
*1981–1986 pintores y escultores españo-
les,* Fundación Caja de Pensiones,
Madrid
*XLII Biennale de Venezia: Ferrán Garcia
Sevilla, Cristina Iglesias, Miquel Navarro,
José Maria Sicilia, Spanish Pavilion,*
Venice
VI Salón de los 16, Museo de Arte
Español Contemporáneo, Madrid
L'attitude, Galeria Cómicos, Lisbon
*VIII Bienal Ciudad de Zamora, Escultura
Ibérica Contemporánea,* Junta de
Castilla y León, Zamora
Escultura sobre la pared, Galeria Juana
de Aizpuru, Madrid

1985 *Christa Dichgans, Lili Dujourie, Marlene
Dumas, Lesley Foxcroft, Kees de Goede,
Frank van Hemert, Cristina Iglesias,
Harald Klingelhöller, Mark Luyten,
Juan Muñoz, Katherine Porter, Juliâo
Sarmento, Barbara Schmidt-Heins,
Gabriele Schmidt-Heins, Didier Ver-
meiren,* Stedelijk Van Abbemuseum,
Eindhoven
Punto y final, Galería Fúcares, Almagro
El desnudo, Galería Juana de Aizpuru,
Madrid

1983–84 *La imagen del animal: Arte prehistórico,
arte contemporáneo,* Caja de Ahorros
y Monte de Piedad, Palacio de las
Alhajas, Madrid; Fundación "La Caixa",
Barcelona

**Bücher und Kataloge zu
Einzelausstellungen I Books and
catalogues for solo exhibitions**

Cristina Iglesias, Arqueologías. Antonio
Cervera Pinto. Portugal: Casa del Bocage, Galería
Municipal de Arte Visuais de Sétubal, 1984

Cristina Iglesias: Sculptures 1984–1987.
Alexandre Melo. Bordeaux: C.A.P.C. Museé d'Art
Contemporain, 1987

Cristina Iglesias. Aurora Garcia und |
and Jiri Svesta. Düsseldorf: Kunstverein für die
Rheinlande und Westfalen, 1988

Cristina Iglesias. Bart Cassiman.
Amsterdam: De Apple Foundation, 1990.

Cristina Iglesias, Esculturas Recentes.
Texte von | Texts by Cristina Iglesias. Lisboa:
Galería Cómicos, 1990

Cristina Iglesias. Ulrich Loock und | and
José Ángel Valente. Bern: Kunsthalle Bern, 1991

Cristina Iglesias. Pepé Espaliú und | and
Loretta Yarlow. Ontario: Art Gallery of York
University, North York, 1992

Cristina Iglesias. XIV Bienal de Venecia.
Aurora García und | and José Ángel Valente.
Barcelona: Ámbit Servicios Editoriales S.A., 1993

Cristina Iglesias. Zdenka Badovinac.
Slovenia: Mala Galerija, Moderna Galerija,
Ljubljana, 1993

Cristina Iglesias. Francisco Jarauta.
San Sebastián; Galería D.V., 1996

Cristina Iglesias: Cinco proyectos.
Javier Maderuelo. Madrid: Fundación Argentaria,
1996

Cristina Iglesias. Nancy Princenthal,
Adrian Searle und | and Barbara María Stafford.
New York: Solomon R. Guggenheim Foundation,
1997

Al otro lado del espejo. Marga Paz.
Madrid: Ediciones El Viso, 1999

Cristina Iglesias. Jennifer Bloomer,
Patricia Falguières, Michael Tarantino und | and
Guy Tosatto. Nîmes; Acte Sud/Carré d'Art –
Musée d'art contemporain de Nîmes, 2000

Cristina Iglesias. Kritisches Lexikon der Gegenwartskunst. Doris von Drathen. München: Weltkunst und Bruckmann, 2002

Cristina Iglesias. Hrsg. von | ed. by Iwona Blazwick. Barcelona: Ediciones Poligrafa, 2002

Kataloge zu ausgewählten Gruppenausstellungen | Catalogues of selected group exhibitions

La imagen del animal: Arte prehistórico, arte contemporáneo. Madrid: Caja de Ahorros and Monte de Piedad, Palacio de las Alhajas, 1983

Christa Dichgans, Lili Dujourie, Marlene Dumas, Lesley Foxcroft, Kees de Goede, Frank van Hemert, Cristina Iglesias, Harald Klingelhöller, Mark Luyten, Juan Muñoz, Katherine Porter, Julião Sarmento, Barbara Schmidt-Heins, Gabriele Schmidt-Heins, Didier Vermeiren. Texte über | Texts on C. I. by Lourdes Iglesias. Eindhoven: Stedelijk Van Abbe-museum, 1985

17 artistas, 17 autonomías. Text von | Text by Marga Paz. Sevilla: Consejería de Cultura de la Junta de Andalucía, 1986

8 de Marzo. Text von | Text by Mar Villaespesa. Málaga: Diputación Provincial, 1986

España en la XLII Bienal de Venecia, 1986. Texte von | Texts by Francisco Calvo Serraller, Marga Paz, Rosa Queralt and Ana Vázquez de Parga. Madrid: Ministerio de Asuntos Exteriores y Ministerio de Cultura, 1986

VI Salón de los 16. Texte von | Texts by Miguel Logroño. Madrid: Museo de Arte Español Contemporáneo, 1986

Beelden en Banieren. Texte von | Texts by R. H. Fuchs und | and Pet de Jonge. Acquoy: Fort Asperen, 1987

Quatriémes ateliers internstionaux des Pays de la Loire. Texte von | Texts by Lynne Cooke und | and Chris Dercon. Abbaye de Fontevraud: FRAC, Pays de la Loire, 1987

Cinq siècles d'art espagnol. Espagne 87:

Dynamiques et Interrogations. Texts by Carmen Gallano. París: ARC, Museè d'Art Moderne de la Ville, 1987

Rosc '88. Texte von | Texts by Aidan Dunne, Olle Granath Rosemarie Mulcahy und | and Angelica Zander Rudenstine. Dublin: Royal Dublin Society, The Guinness Hop Store and the Royal Hospital Kilmainham, 1988

Three spanish artists: Cristina Iglesias, Pello Irazu y Fernando Sinaga. Texte von | Texts by Aurora García. Seattle: Donald Young Gallery, 1988

Artisti spagnoli contemporanei. Texte von | Texts by Dan Cameron, Mariano Navarro und | and Kevin Power. Milán: Rotonda di Via Besana and Studio Marconi, 1988

Jeunes sculptures espagnols: au ras du sol, le dos au mur. Fernando Huici. Madrid: Ministerio de Cultura, 1989

Spain Art today. Miguel Fernández Cid. Takanawa: Museum of Modern Art, 1989

Psychological Abstraction. Texts by Jeffrey Deitch. Athens: DESTE Foundation for Contemporary Art, 1989

The Eighth Biennale of Sydney: The Readymade Boomerang: Certain relations in Twentieth century Art. Text by Cristina Iglesias. Sydney: Art Gallery of New South Wales, 1990

Hacia el paisaje/Towards the landscape. Texts by Aurora García und | and Denys Zacharopoulos. Las Palmas: Centro Atlántico de Arte Moderno, 1990

Metropolis. Texte von | Texts by Jeffrey Deitch, Wolfgang Max Faust, Vilém Flusser, Boris Grouys, Jenny Holzer, Christos M. Joachimides, Dietmar Kamper, Achille Bonito Oliva, Norman Rosenthal, Christoph Tannert and Paul Virilo. New York: Rizzoli International Publications, INC., 1990

Espacio mental. Text von | Text by Bart Cassiman. Valencia: IVAM Centre Julio González, 1991

*Before and after enthusiasm,
1972–1992.* Text von | Text by José Luis Brea,
conversation with Cristina Iglesias. Amsterdam:
KunstRai, 1992

*Los ochenta en la colección de la
Fundación La Caixa.* Texte von | Texts by Mariano
Navarro, Kevin Power und | and Evelyn Weiss.
Barcelona: Fundació "La Caixa", 1992

Últimos días/The Last days. Texte von |
Texts by Juan Vicente Allaga, José Luis Brea,
Massimo Cacciari, Dan Cameron, Manuel Clot
und | and Francisco Jarauta. Madrid: Gran Vía
S.A., 1992

Pasajes: Actualidad del Arte Español.
(Pabellón de España, Exposición Universal de
Sevilla 1992). Text von | Text by Teresa Blanch
und | and José Luis Brea. Madrid: Editorial Electa,
1992

*Colección del IVAM. Adquisiciones
1985–1992.* Valencia: IVAM Centre Julio González,
1992

*Tropismes, Collecció d'Art Contemporani
Fundació "La Caixa".* Texte von | Texts by Rosa
Queralt, Dan Cameron und | and Nimfa Bisbe.
Barcelona: Fundació "La Caixa", 1992

*Escultura española actual: Una
generación para un fin de siglo.* Francisco Calvo
Serraller. Madrid: Fundación Lugar, 1992

Juxtaposition. Texte von | Texts by
Mikkel Borgh und | and John Peter Nielsson.
Copenhagen: Chalottenborg, 1993

*The sublime Void (On the Memory of
Imagination).* Texte von | Texts by Bart Cassi-
man. Antwerp: Koninklijk Museum voor Schone
Kunster, 1993

*La voce del genere. Cristina Iglesias,
Eva Lootz y Soledad Sevilla.* Text von | Text by
Mar Villaespesa. Roma: Instituto Cervantes,
1994

Malpaís. Grabados y monotipos. Text
by Andrés Sánchez Robayna. Lanzarote: Galería-
taller Línea, 1994

*Some Notes on Nothing and the Silence
of Works of Art: Lili Dujourie, Pepe Espaliú,
Cristina Iglesias.* Texte von | Texts by Michael
Newman. London: Chisenhale Gallery, 1995

Gravity's Angel. Texte von | Texts by
Penelope Curtis. Leeds: Henry Moore
Foundation, 1995

Carnegie International 1995. Pittsburgh:
The Canegie Museum of Art, 1995

*Ten years of the foundation of the
Kunsthalle Bern.* Bern: Kunsthalle Bern, 1997

Escultura española actual. Text von |
Text by Francisco Calvo Serraller. Madrid: Galería
Malborough, 1997

En la piel del toro. Texte von | Texts by
Aurora García und | and Joaqim Manuel
Magalhâes. Madrid: Museo Nacional Centro de
Arte Reina Sofía, 1997

*Damenwahl, Cristina Iglesias, Olaf
Metzel.* Gespräch zwischen | Conversation bet-
ween Cristina Iglesias, Ursula Kuhn, Olaf Metzel
und | and Matthias Winzen. Munich: Siemens
Kulturprogramm, 1999

North and South transcultural visions.
Wroclaw: Mediterranean Foundation, 1999

Co-laboraciones Arquitectos- Artistas.
Texte von | Texts by Lius Fernández-Galiano
and Mark Wigley. Lisboa: Parque Expo'98, S.A.,
2000

Dialog, Kunst im Pavillon. Text von |
Text by Victor de Río. Hannover: State Society of
Hannover, 2000

Enclosed and Exchanted. Texte von |
Texts by Kerry Brougher und | and Michael
Tarantino. Oxford: Museum of Contemporain
Art, 2000

Dialogue Ininterrompu. Nantes:
Éditions MeMo. Musée des Beaux Arts, 2001
Encrucijada. Reflexiones sobre la pintura actual.
Madrid: Consejería de Cultura de la Comunidad
de Madrid, 2001

*La noche. Imágenes de la noche en
el arte español. 1981–2001.* Text von | Text by
José María Parreño. Segovia: Museo de Arte
Contemporáneo Esteban Vicente, 2001

**Ausgewählte Artikel und Interviews |
Selected articles and interviews**

Sol Alameda. "Cristina Iglesias".
In: *El País Semanal*, n° 1.272, 11 February 2001,
S. | p. 53–65.

Francisco Calvo Serraller." Una revela-
ción convincente". In: *El País*, 20 October 1984.

Francisco Calvo Serraller. "La Nouvelle
sculpture espagnole". In: *Artpress*, n° 117,
September 1987, S. | p. 17–20.

Francisco Calvo Serraller. "Aconteci-
miento espacial". In: *Arte y Parte*, n° 39, 2002.

Robin Cembalest. "Learning to absorb
the shock of the new". In: *Artnews* 88, n° 7,
New York, September 1989, S. | p. 121–131.

Miguel Fernández-Cid. "¿ A tiempo
para la escultura?". In: *Lápiz*, n° 36, Madrid,
October 1986.

Eric Fredericksen. "Cristina Iglesias
at Donald Young: Feminine Mystiche. In: *The
Stranger Weekly* 5, n° 27, Seattle 1996, S. | p. 20.

Alan G. Artner. "At the galleries: Ex-
ploring the flower of morality: Cristina Iglesias,
Pello Irazu, Fernand Sinaga". In: *Chicago Tribune*,
20 October, 1988, S. | p. 12.

Jamey Gambrell. "Five from Spain".
In: *Art in America* 9, n° 75, New York, September
1987, S. | p. 160–171.

Aurora García. "Galería Marga Paz,
Madrid". In: *Art Forum*, n° 26, New York, February
1988, S. | p. 155–156.

Hervé Gauville. "Iglesias, le plein des
sens". In: *Libération*, 6 May 2000.

Simon Grant. "Lili Dujourie/Pepe
Espaliú/Cristina Iglesias". In: Art Monthly, n° 191,
noviembre 1995, S. | p. 35–37.

Catherine Grout. "Cristina Iglesias, Juan
Muñoz: Sculptures". In: *Artstudio*, n° 14, Autumn
1989, S. | p. 110–117.

Regina Hackett. "Iglesias Mind-
Bending Murals and Sculptures Take Hold in
US". In: *Seattle Post Intelligencer*, Seattle, 15
March, 1996.

Sylvaine Hansel. "Berufung auf die
eigne Tradition". In: *Weltkunst* 60, n° 9, Munich,
May 1990.

José Jímenez. "Muros de ensueño".
In: *El Mundo*, 4 March, 2000.

Matthew Kangas. "Seattle: Cristina
Iglesias, Donald Young Gallery". In: *Sculpture*,
n° 15, Washington, July–August 1996.

Jutta Koeter, Diederichsen Dietrich.
"Jutta and Dietrich go to Spain: Spanish Art and
Culture view from Madrid". In: *Artscribe Internacional* n° 59, London, September–October
1986.

Claire Lieberman. "Stone Mystery or
Malaise?". *Sculptors on Sculpture*, vol. 17, n° 2,
February, 1988.

Alexandre Mélo. "Cristina Iglesias,
a free exercise of intelligence". In: *Flash Art*,
Milan, n° 138, Milan, January-February 1988,
S. | p. 91–92.

Alexandre Mélo. "Cristina Iglesias
oeuvres en ciment". In: *Le Journal des Lettres*,
September 1984.

Alexandre Mélo. "Galería Cómicos,
Lisbon". In: *Artforum*, n° 29, May 1991, S. | p. 157.

Alicia Murria. "Venezia: La Biennale".
In: *Lápiz*, vol. 11, n° 93, May 1993, S. | p. 20–23.

"Neue Ankäufe der Stifung Kunsthalle
Bern". In: Berner Kunstmittelungen, n° 281,
September-October 1991, S. | p. 11–13.

Rosa Olivares, Carlos Jímenez, Alicia
Murria, Celia Montolio. "Bienal de Venecia".
In: *Lápiz*, vol. 11, n° 94, January–February 1996,
S. | p. 19–21.

Marga Paz. "Memoria desordenada.
Cristina Iglesias and Caterina Borelli". In:
El Europeo, n° 49, Spring 1994.

Ángel L. Pérez Villén. "La vanitas
neobarroca". In: *Lápiz*, vol. 10, n° 87, May–June
1992, S. | p. 64–67.

Nancy Proctor. "Playing to the gallery".
In: *Women's Art Magazine*, n° 68, January–
February 1996, S. | p. 19–21.

30

Uta M. Reindl. "Kunstlerporträts: Cristina Iglesias". In: *Kunstforum International*, n° 94, Aprill–May 1988, S. | p. 132–135.

Barbara Probst Solomon. "Out of the shadows: Art in Post Franco Spain". In: *Artnews*, vol. 86, n° 86, October 1987, S. | p. 120–124.

George Stoltz. "Fast Forward (Nineteen Artists Whose Works are Gaining Recognition)". In: *Artnews*, vol. 92, n° 9, November 1993, S. | p. 130–131.

George Stoltz. "Cristina Iglesias and Juan Muñoz". In: *The New York Times*, 15 June 1997.

Andrés Sánchez Robayna. "Signos de la cultura española contemporánea". In: *Quimera*, n° 163, November 1997.

Michael Tarantino. "Joost Declerq, Gante". In: *Artforum*, n° 27, February 1989, S. | p. 146.

V.V.A.A. "La nouvelle sculpture espagnole". In: *Art Press*, n° 117, París, September 1987, S. | p. 17–20.

Helena Vasconcelos. "Entrevista con Cristina Iglesias". In: *Figura*, n. 7–8, Printemps 1986, S. | p. 51–53.

Videos

Memoria desordenada. Caterina Borelli, 1996 (28 min.)

Guided Tour. Caterina Borelli and Cristina Iglesias, 1999–2002

Ausstellung | Exhibition:

DC: Cristina Iglesias, Drei hängende Korridore |
Three Suspended Corridors
Museum Ludwig, Köln

25. März 2005 – 25. Juni 2006
25 March 2005 – 25 June 2005

Für ihre Unterstützung der Ausstellung danken wir dem
AC: / DC: Förderkreis | For their support of the exhibition
we would like to thank the AC: / DC: Group of Patrons

Bach, Langheid & Dallmayr, Rechtanwälte

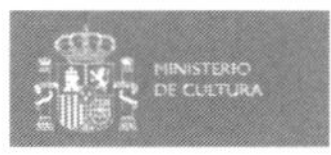 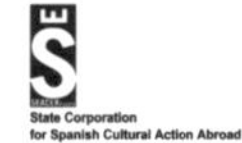

Herausgeber | Editors: Ulrich Wilmes, Kasper König

Assistenten | Assistents: Ana Fernández-Cid,
Paola Malavassi

Besonderer Dank an | Special Thanks to:
Clara Beatriz Antunez
Juana Jiminez
Julián López
Angel Jorquer Luna
José Antonio Sotelo

© 2006 Cristina Iglesias,
Autoren | Authors, Museum Ludwig, Köln
und | and Verlag der Buchhandlung
Walther König, Köln

Insert: Cristina Iglesias

Übersetzung | Translation: Alison Shamrock

Installationsansichten | Installation views,
Museum Ludwig (Seite | page 4, 10/11, 13, 22/23):
Attilio Maranzano

Fotografie | Photography: Kristien Daem, Luis Asin,
Attilio Maranzano, Georges Méguerdichian

Lithografie | Lithography: Farbanalyse, Köln

Gestaltung | Design: Silke Fahnert, Uwe Koch, Köln
Yvonne Quirmbach (Logo)

Herstellung | Production: Fries Printmedien, Köln

Die Deutsche Bibliothek – CIP-Einheitsaufnahme
Ein Titelsatz für diese Publikation ist bei
Der Deutschen Bibliothek erhältlich

Distribution outside Europe:

D. A. P. / Distributed Art Publishers, New York
155 Sixth Avenue, New York, NY 10013
Tel 212-627-1999 Fax 212-627-9484

ISBN 3-86560-086-7   Printed in Germany

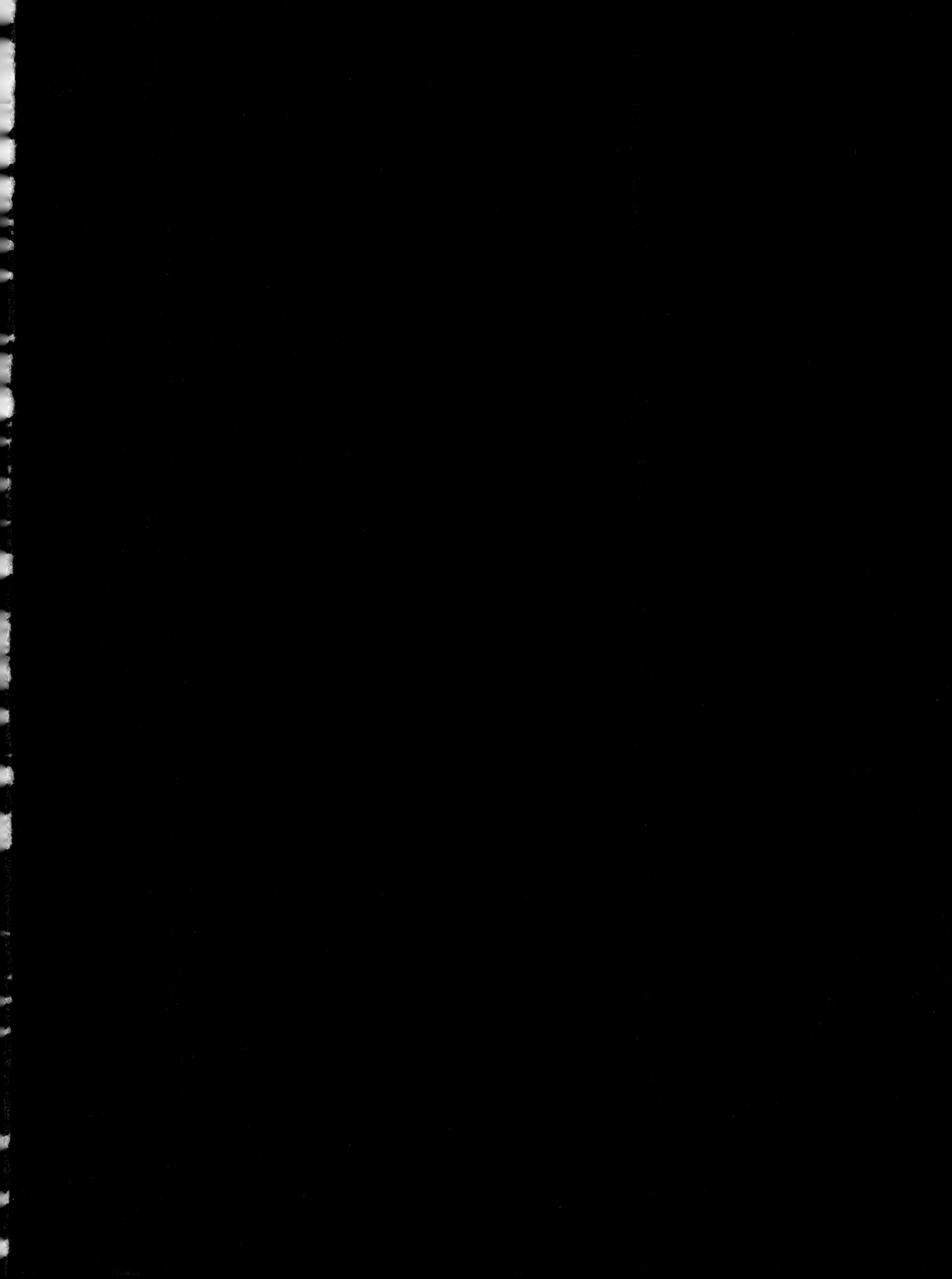